W9-ARB-223

A PICTORIAL HISTORY
OF THE WORLD'S GREATEST
CHILD STAR

# Shirley Temple

## A Pictorial History of the World's Greatest Child Star

written & designed by
Rita Dubas

SOUTH HUNTINGTON
PUBLIC LIBRARY
HUNTINGTON STATION, NY 11746

APPLAUSE THEATRE & CINEMA BOOKS · · NEW YORK

Shirley Temple: A Pictorial History of the World's Greatest Child Star
By Rita Dubas

Copyright © 2006 Rita Dubas
All rights reserved

No part of this publication may be reproduced or transmitted in any form or by any means, electronic or mechanical, including photocopy, recording or any other information storage or retrieval system now known or to be invented, without permission in writing from the publisher, except by a reviewer who wishes to quote brief passages in connection with a review written for inclusion in a magazine, newspaper, or broadcast.

The films *Stand Up and Cheer!, Baby Take A Bow, Bright Eyes, The Little Colonel, Our Little Girl, Curly Top, The Littlest Rebel, Captain January, The Poor Little Rich Girl, Dimples, Stowaway, Wee Willie Winkie, Heidi, Rebecca of Sunnybrook Farm, Little Miss Broadway, Just Around the Corner, The Little Princess, Susannah of the Mounties, The Blue Bird* and *Young People* are copyright © Twentieth Century Fox. The films *Little Miss Marker* and *Now and Forever* are copyright © Paramount Pictures, Inc.

This book is a work of scholarship, unrelated to any trademark status and represents no venture of any of the above-mentioned companies.
Referential usage of the name Shirley Temple, any of her films and related images is not to be construed as a challenge to any trademark status.

All photographs and memorabilia in this book are from the personal collection of the author.

Book design by Rita Dubas.
The text of this book was set in Bitstream Schneidler, designed by F.H.E. Schneidler for the Bauer type foundry in 1936; the headings were set in a modified version of Bitstream Liorah, designed by Holly Goldsmith in 2000; and the subheads set in Futura Serie® BQ, a digital redesign of the well-known 1930 Futura typeface by Dieter Hofrichter for the Berthold type foundry in 2000.

Library of Congress Cataloging-in-Publication Data:
Dubas, Rita.
Shirley Temple : a pictorial history of the world's greatest child star /
written & designed by Rita Dubas.
p. cm.
ISBN-13: 978-1-55783-672-4 (hardcover)
ISBN-10: 1-55783-672-8 (hardcover)
1. Temple, Shirley, 1928---Pictorial works. 2. Temple, Shirley, 1928-
--Collectibles. 3. Motion picture actors and actresses--United States--
Biography--Pictorial works. I. Title.

PN2287.T33D83 2006
791.4302'8092--dc22
[B]
2006020244

Applause Theatre & Cinema Books
19 West 21st Street, Suite 201
New York, NY 10010
Phone:(212)575-9265
Fax:(212)575-9270
Email: info@applausepub.com
Internet: www.applausepub.com
Applause books are available through your local bookstore, or you may order at www.applausepub.com
or call Music Dispatch at 800-637-2852

Sales & Distribution

North America:
Hal Leonard Corp.
7777 West Bluemound Road
P. O. Box 13819
Milwaukee, WI 53213
Phone: (414) 774-3630
Fax: (414) 774-3259

Europe:
Roundhouse Publishing Ltd.
Millstone, Limers Lane
Northam, North Devon EX 39 2RG
Phone: (0) 1237-474-474
Fax: (0) 1237-474-774
Email: roundhouse.group@ukgateway.net
Internet: www.halleonard.com
Email: halinfo@halleonard.com

Printed in China through Colorcraft Ltd, HongKong.

# Contents

# Wonder Tot

There is no official published birth announcement for a child born at the Santa Monica Hospital on April 23, 1928 at 9:00 p.m. If one existed, it would read as follows:

"A girl, born to Mrs. Gertrude Kreiger Temple of 948 24th Street, Santa Monica. Her parents have named her Shirley Jane. George Temple, proud father, prepared for the birth in advance by having his tonsils removed, thereby acknowledging an old wives tale recommending this procedure to produce a baby girl. The Temples have two sons, "Sonny" and Jack, and hoped for a daughter to complete their family. Mrs. Temple is a homemaker; Mr. Temple is employed as a manager at the Vermont Avenue branch of the California Bank. Their new arrival has a good disposition, is in good health, will have a salary by the time she's three, and in a little over six years will be the most recognizable celebrity in the world."

By the time Shirley joined the Temple family, brothers Sonny (George Jr.) and Jack were 12 and 14, old enough to start distancing themselves from Mom and secure enough to enjoy having a kid sister to impress, tease or dismiss as older brothers will. Mrs. Temple was able to concentrate on Shirley, and kept a keen eye on her new baby's development and interests. This nurturing atmosphere was the basis for a family dynamic that surrounded Shirley throughout her childhood: she and her mother became a team and her brothers kept her grounded. Shirley's father, far from playing second fiddle to his daughter and wife, was very visible in the background. A jovial man whom Shirley resembled, he beamed with pride while supporting Mrs. Temple in her daily responsibility of keeping Shirley safe and sane. "Although it takes Daddy a week to earn what his five-year-old daughter makes in a single day, life in the Temple home—as in the typical American home—revolves about Dad," reported a

**Opposite: Shirley Jane Temple and mom Gertrude in their sunny Santa Monica garden, circa 1931. Shirley was about three years old and on the brink of her film career in this family snapshot. Below: A beaded pincushion from 1928—the correct year of Shirley's birth.**

**Top: Shirley and big brother Jack Temple at the Matsonia Lines passenger dock before she and her family sailed for Hawaii in 1935. Center: Brother George Jr. (Sonny) in Hawaii on the same trip. Above: Dad George Temple outside the California Bank in the mid-1950s.**

**Opposite: Shirley stands in her playpen in the front yard of the Temple home, circa 1929.**

1935 Russell Birdwell column. "No more fuss is made over [Shirley] than the ordinary adoration that is given any little girl in a household . . ."

Gertrude Temple had always loved to dance, and while expecting, influenced her future child through exposure to music and the arts. Instinctively positive that her baby was a girl, she was hopeful that her offspring would also learn to enjoy dancing. While Shirley was barely standing in her playpen, the nearby radio was constantly tuned to popular music. Mrs. Temple was aware that Shirley was clinging to the railing, energetically swaying to the beat. Much later, she would recall in interviews that as a toddler, Shirley would run on her toes rather than walk, as if she were dancing. Shirley herself doesn't remember anything that extraordinary about an early display of talent; she was simply responding to the music as she watched her mother dance to the tunes. However Shirley's ability revealed itself, Mrs. Temple eventually took some of the household money and enrolled her three-year-old daughter at the Santa Monica branch of the Meglin Dance Studio for fifty cents a week.

The studio was owned by Ethel Meglin, one of George Temple's banking customers and a formidable woman who became renowned for the early training of several child entertainers including Shirley, Judy Garland and actress Jane Withers (*Bright Eyes,* 1934; *Ginger,* 1935). While a few later articles hinted that Meglin's was part of Mrs. Temple's master plan to make Shirley a star, she never actively promoted her child as many of the other mothers did. It was clear that Shirley, with her crown of Botticelli curls, stood out in the preschool crowd without the aid of frilly outfits or over-the-top coiffures. Her rapid mastering of intricate dance steps added to her charm, and within a few months she became one of the "Famous Meglin Kiddie" troupe. Despite Shirley's progress, Mrs. Temple was unaware that a Hollywood studio representative was scheduled to visit the class to audition prospective toddlers for a new series of short films. On the designated day, Mrs. Temple showed up as usual with Shirley wearing a plain blue rehearsal tog, while the other children were dressed to the nines. Embarrassed, Mrs. Temple offered to take Shirley home and change her outfit. One of the instructors intervened and asked them to stay. Shirley marched into the main hall with the other kids and became aware that a strange man was offhandedly staring at her. She promptly hid in the only spot she could find. The talent scout had noticed her immediately and, as went the pivotal part of the Shirley Temple legend, opted for "the one behind the piano."

The scout was from Educational Pictures, a small independent studio producing a wide range of featurettes. Educational's latest concept was designed to compete with the highly popular *Our Gang*

Mrs. Temple signed with a local photographer to document Shirley's growth from the time she was a baby until the age of six. By that time, Shirley was one of the world's most photographed celebrities and such an arrangement was moot. The "yard-long" vignette picture, above, shows Shirley from eighteen months through age four; this composite image was included with Mrs. Temple's original photography studio contract.

series. The *Baby Burlesks* would showcase toddlers playing adult stars in takeoffs on popular films of the day. The children, while not required to appear as miniature adults, had mature voices dubbed over their own as the series' main gimmick. Adding to the illusion were garments that featured full costumes on top and diapers clasped with oversized brass safety pins on the bottom. Shirley was quickly signed as a lead "Baby Star" at ten dollars per working day, stunning the Temples. The rapid turn of events for their three-year-old included Mrs. Temple, who was offered five dollars a day to supervise Shirley on the set. In her first bid to monitor Shirley's wellbeing, she determined that the idea of a real diaper was inappropriate for a child a tad too old to wear one. Instead, Mrs. Temple adopted the job of designing and sewing Shirley's wardrobe as modified tap dance costumes, incorporating the trademark safety pin.

**Opposite: Four-year-old Shirley's first "head shot," taken by United Studios in 1932.**

**Above right: Baby Shirley Jane Temple and two diapered doughboys in the first released *Baby Burlesk* short *War Babies*. Below: Two of Shirley's original oversized diaper pins, part of her *Burlesk* wardrobe. The smaller of the two was worn only in the publicity still above—for the balance of the series, Shirley wore the same large pin as the rest of the cast. Ethel Meglin requested the two pins and photograph for her dance studio archives in 1936.**

The first film scheduled was *Runt Page,* a spoof of *The Front Page* and shot in December, 1931. The short opens with a sleepy Shirley seated in a high chair, listening to her parents and their friends critique the movie they saw the night before. She dozes off and dreams about a toddler reenactment of one of the scenes, walking on as one of the baby actors' girlfriends in the last few frames. The film was not released, possibly because the sound of adult voices was too distracting out of the mouths of toddlers (the overall effect is un-synched and bizarre). The series was shelved until the concept was retooled, and it seemed Shirley's short-lived Hollywood career was over.

Back at Meglin's, Shirley added vocal lessons to her expanding repertoire. In December, 1932 four-year-old Shirley would make her first appearance on stage at a gala benefit for the Unemployed Citizens League of Santa Monica with no less a personality than the wildly popular Western star, Will Rogers.

"Thursday night Shirley received a big ovation at the benefit show," raved the *Santa Monica Evening Outlook.* "Will Rogers, master of ceremonies, praised her singing and tap dancing. At the conclusion of her set, the illustrious humorist joined her in the dance and the two left the stage with the audience thundering applause." The article went on to mention Shirley's affiliation with the local Meglin studio, and the series of short films she was currently filming in Hollywood.

United Studios
Hollywood

Hollywood, California

**Baby Stars Confer to Elect Ice Cream Favorite Sweet**



Birthday cake comes first among childish preferences for sweets, according to these film youngsters. Especially ice cream cake, full of strawberry ice cream, like the pictured Sunfreze cake. SHIRLEY TEMPLE, top left, youngest leading lady in pictures, featured in Jack Hays' "Baby Burlesks" at Educational Pictures, casts her vote for the Sunfreze ice cream, with yummy syrup on the bottom. Upper right, this demure ingenue entertains some of her supporting cast, including, left to right, DANIEL BOONE, great-grandchild of the pioneer; MARILYN MILNER, and GEORGE SMITH. Lower right, a delicious scene from "Polly Tix in Washington," another Educational Picture featuring the baby stars.

Educational, realizing Shirley's potential, had called on her when the *Baby Burlesks* resumed filming in the summer of 1932. Five months had passed since *Runt Page*, and by this time, producer Jack Hays had signed Shirley to a new contract that allowed him to loan her out for films, radio and stage shows for a period of two years. The newly revamped *Burlesks* allowed its young actors to recite their lines in their own voices, and the series found an eager distributor. Simple singing and dancing numbers were created for "Baby Shirley Jane Temple," who was promoted as the troupe's leading lady. Her first on-screen lines were spoken in the short *War Babies,* a spoof on *What Price Glory*—in French! Shirley, starring as a dance-hall chanteuse, wiggled her shoulders, batted her eyes and phonetically flirted with a toddler soldier: *"Me, mon cher¿"* Six other *Burlesk* shorts were filmed in succession over the next several months. Production quality improved with each short, but most of the kids still tended to shout their lines at the microphone. Shirley became the standout by singing, dancing and skillfully mimicking performers such as Marlene Dietrich. She was featured front and center in all publicity photos and trade notices, and singled out for ad campaigns for Sunfreze ice cream and Agfa film. Despite Hays' promotional efforts, the *Burlesks* were never as successful as its superior rival, *Our Gang.* Educational shut the series down in early 1933, with its place in film history solidly on the shoulders of its future superstar, Baby Shirley Jane.

Shirley's experience left her with a sense of teamwork, concentration and pure hard work—though carefully monitored by her mother who was always with her on the set. Jack Hays and director Charles Lamont instilled their young cast with the maxim "Time is money," and Shirley, not yet five, carried that philosophy into the next segment of her career. Although the later publicity legend suggested that Shirley had simply exploded on to the screen after her first appearance in a feature film, she was honing her skills in bit parts, walk-ons and other short films after the *Burlesks* ended. Hays had let no opportunity slip by in exercising his option to loan out his star player. She made an appearance as a flower girl at a bridal fashion show with the Wampas Baby Stars (a troupe of young ingénues including Ginger Rogers), and entertained at the annual Shrine Circus in Los Angeles. Shirley also appeared in no less than ten films and

MAY 15, 1932. [PART III.]

DISC INSTRUCTION LATE INNOVATION

SHIRLEY TEMPLE

**Above left: An advertorial piece featuring the Baby Stars and their lead ingenue for Sunfreze Ice Cream from the *Hollywood Citizen News,* July 6, 1933. Above: Baby Shirley promotes the latest innovation in dance discs in the Los Angeles *Times.***

**Opposite: Cecilia Parker photographs Shirley and dog star Prince Barry for Agfa Film in 1932.**

Shirley as Morelegs Sweetrick (Marlene Dietrich) sang "We Just Couldn't Say Goodbye" in the *Baby Burlesk* short *Kid' in' Hollywood* (1932). This elaborate, spangled outfit was made by Mrs. Temple. Opposite: A sampling of the short subjects made by Educational Pictures in which Shirley had a role. Below: An ad from the 1933 edition of the *Film Daily Yearbook* placed by producer Jack Hays. Hays would eventually sue the Temple family for a percentage of Shirley's earnings, claiming that their contract was never properly terminated after he declared bankruptcy. He lost.

*Polly Tix in Washington* (1932).

*Pie-Covered Wagon* (1932).

*Kid in Africa* (1932).

*Managed Money*, one of the *Frolics of Youth* (1933).

*Kid in Africa* (1932).

*Pardon My Pups*, one of the *Frolics of Youth* with Junior Coughlin (1933).

*Baby Burlesk* cast and crew, 1932.

*The Kid's Last Fight* (1932).

With Jack Hays and Baby Star Georgie Smith, 1932.

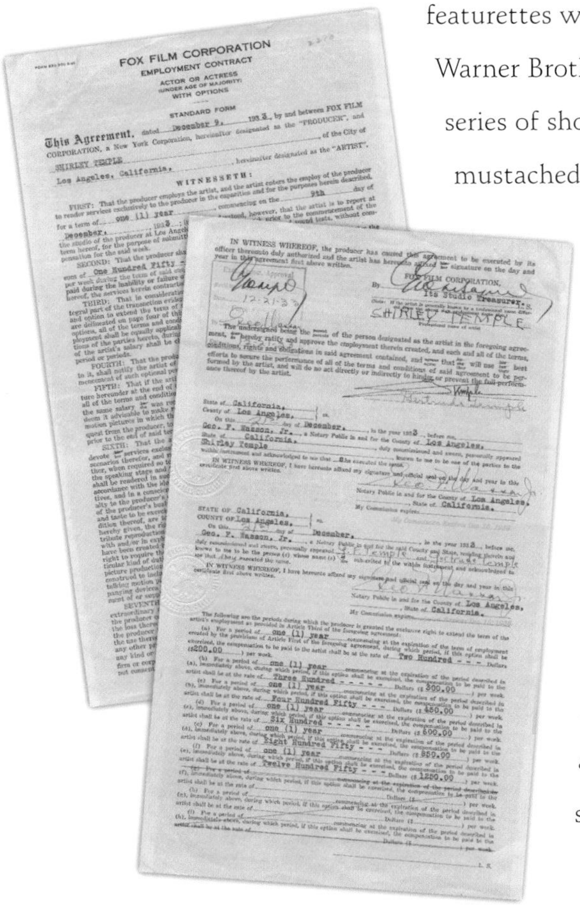

featurettes within the year, on loan to such studios as Universal, Paramount, Warner Brothers and her future professional home, Fox Films. She made another series of shorts, the *Frolics of Youth,* for Educational, and starred with popular, mustached comedian Andy Clyde in the short *Dora's Dunking Doughnuts.* She had a speaking role in the screen version of Zane Grey's *To the Last Man* with Randolph Scott. She acted with Spencer Tracy and Alice Faye in *Now I'll Tell,* in *Carolina* with Janet Gaynor, and in *Change of Heart* with Charles Farrell. These mega-stars of the early 1930s would cross paths with Shirley again, when she was the top box office star in movies.

By late 1933, Jack Hays declared personal bankruptcy, leaving Shirley without a self-proclaimed agent or career. She had already spent half her life in the film industry. Quiet for the first time in months, she reportedly attended kindergarten at the end of her block and played with the regular Santa Monica neighborhood kids. Her specialty was mudpies garnished with seaweed.

Shortly after her sudden retirement, Shirley and her family were attending a preview of her latest *Frolics of Youth* short, *What to Do?,* at a Los Angeles theater. Much like her discovery at Meglin's, a stranger observed her from a distance and then asked where her mother was. Jay Gorney was a songwriter with Fox Films, and thought he recognized the *Frolics* starlet in the theater lobby. Although Shirley had already worked at Fox, and it's logical that the casting office was keeping an eye on her as a potential player, legend has it that Mrs. Temple agreed to bring Shirley to the studio to be tested for a future Depression-busting musical extravaganza, *Fox Follies.* At this point, the studio was in desperate financial shape.

Shirley appeared only briefly in the film, retitled *Stand Up and Cheer!,* released in the spring of 1934. Before filming began in December 1933, she and her parents signed two revisions of her first contract with Fox Films for a salary of $150 a week. There was a provision for Mrs. Temple to act again as her guardian on the set for $10 a day. When Shirley became an established box office success, her weekly salary would rise more than tenfold. In contrast, the average wage for a working adult at the time hovered around $20 a week.

**The seven-year Fox contract signed by the Temples and Shirley, dated December 9, 1933. This version guaranteed $150 per working week, with increases each year up to $1250 per week if the contract was renewed. Never before published, later publicity claimed that Shirley signed this contract with a sweeping "X" since she was "too young to write."**

**Opposite: The universal image of Shirley in the red-dotted dress from *Stand Up and Cheer!*—her best-known film frock. Inset: Shirley, screen daddy James Dunn and chorus girls in the film's smash "Baby Take A Bow" sequence.**

Fox realized they had a perfect combination of concentration, talent and personality in Shirley, but had no hint of the audience reaction to come. It was later reported that she was hired to replace another little girl in the musical number "Baby Take A Bow," whom Jay Gorney felt too artificial and mature beyond her years to sing the lyrics convincingly. The movie overall was a tedious mishmash of loosely strung scenes revolving around a governmental Department of Amusement designed to combat the Depression. Popular stars of the moment, such as John Boles and Aunt Jemima, appeared in various tuneful cameos. When Shirley finally appeared, larger-than-life on the screen in a flouncy, dotted dancing dress, audiences took notice. Her years of dancing and singing culminated in a few glowing screen minutes as she danced and sang in front of a line of chorus girls trying to musically flirt with her tall, dapper screen daddy, James Dunn. She kept in rapid step with him, curls flying and arms waving. It was a visual that would be forever associated with Shirley. Theater patrons went wild, and box office receipts for the struggling film company began to rise.

**Opposite: A dramatic operating room scene from *Little Miss Marker*. Shirley's character, thrown from her "charger" (the thoroughbred given to her by the racetrack mob), is saved by a transfusion from gangster boss Big Steve (Charles Bickford), shown kneeling over the table.**

This was the second rapid change in the life of the Temple family. Fox promoted Shirley as "the find of the year," and shaved a year off her age to make their new discovery seem even more miraculous. While the studio tried to plan new projects for her, they loaned Shirley to Paramount to audition for the plum role of "Marky" in Damon Runyon's classic racetrack story, *Little Miss Marker.* It was an effortless way to test the type of formula in which Shirley's personality would click.

*Little Miss Marker* is one of Shirley's best childhood films, and the one in which she proved she could hold her own with an established ensemble cast. Starring with Adolphe Menjou, Dorothy Dell and a delectable array of character actors, Shirley played the role of a little girl left as a hold or "marker" for a bet by her father, who commits suicide after losing the fixed race. Menjou as Sorrowful Jones, an Oscar Madison-like bookie, takes Shirley in and she eventually reforms the entire ragtag crew of gangsters with her straightforward innocence and her love for the King Arthur tale of "knights and their ladies fair." Shirley was allowed to truly act and not rely on singing and dancing; high points in the film were reciting her bedtime prayers for the first time while a reflective Menjou tells her what to say, a dramatic scene in an operating room and a controversial spate of "cuss" words—it was unheard of at the time for a child to spout "Nix to that!" and "Scram!" on the screen. Again, audiences were entranced by Shirley, demanding the film's holdover for an unprecedented three weeks in New York.

**Shirley's screen father (Edward Earle, left) deposits her as an I.O.U. for a racetrack bet with unwilling bookie Sorrowful Jones (Adolphe Menjou, right).**

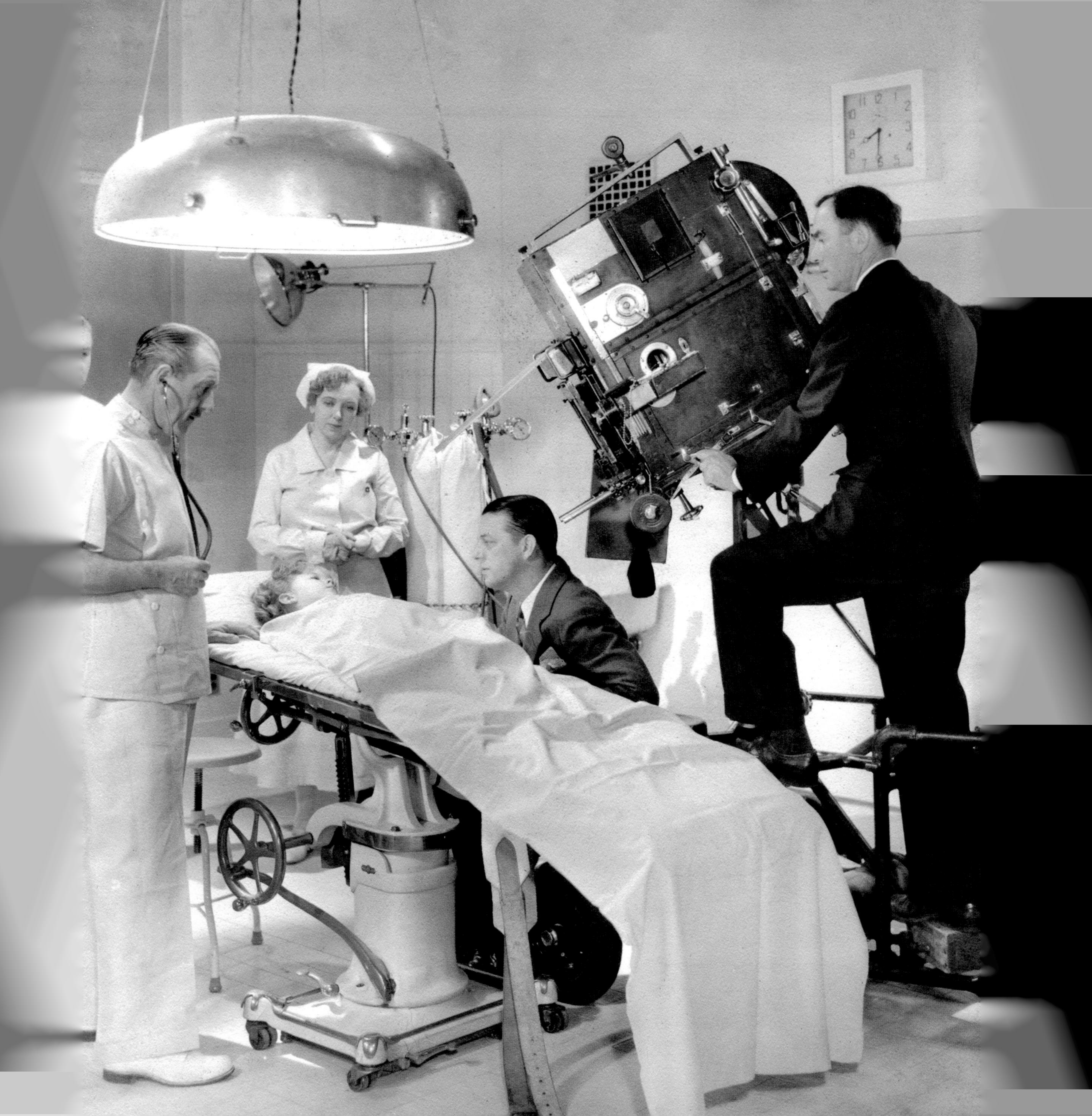

**Opposite: An angelic pose from one of Shirley's first portrait sittings for Fox in early 1934.**

*Angel Face,* a story in the *Little Miss Marker* genre (showgirl Alice Faye adopts orphan Shirley), was developed and dropped by Fox in early 1934. Instead, they opted for *Baby Take a Bow,* another child-reforms-criminal storyline that re-teamed Shirley with *Stand Up and Cheer!* co-star James Dunn. Singing and dancing were added to show off Shirley's range, but the villain of the screenplay was far more threatening than the comedic stereotypes of *Marker.* Similar to the child-in-peril formula used for silent film stars, Shirley was abducted at gunpoint in one scene. Audiences loved her, but began to protest the drastic storylines. She was loaned back to Paramount for *Now and Forever,* a similar reform story starring Gary Cooper and Carole Lombard. The film's last scene— a despondent Cooper drives his car off a cliff after giving Shirley's character up for adoption—had to be refilmed in favor of a happy ending at the request of preview crowds. After hearing the reactions of the public to the contrast of Shirley's roles versus the seamy side of society, Fox had to rethink ways to market their "biggest little star."

By the fall of 1934, Shirley was becoming a national obsession, captivating the country with a dynamic combination of personality, self-reliance and optimism—the perfect outlet for a public in the grips of the Great Depression. Far from being a one-dimensional sweetness and light character, Shirley was an independent kid who commanded a scene with purpose ("Shirley Temple struts!" remarked a *Photoplay Magazine* columnist later in Shirley's career. "She is the only actress unafraid. La Temple can be tender and innocently childish, or she can strut across the set and go into her song and dance. The lass has a martial spirit . . ."). Her confidence contrasted perfectly with the overburdened adult characters of her films, pointing the way to a clear solution to any issue. Her acting appeared spontaneous and natural, while reflecting a real joy in her hard work. The concept of a little girl leading adults was a breath of fresh air during a period when films were turned out with the frequency of today's television series. More than simply "entertainment," the majority of film audiences regarded the release of a movie with their favorite star as a major event. Shirley's films provided an outlet for a society dealing with economic and environmental stress (dust storms in the Midwest, major floods in the East), and the undercurrent of a future war in Europe. If Shirley's characters could muddle their way out of difficult situations with spirit, then there was hope for everyone else.

**Shirley and Gary Cooper in *Now and Forever.* Bottom: Shirley is carried over rooftops by gun-toting Trigger Stone (Ralf Harolde) in *Baby Take A Bow.* Although she wasn't depicted as harmed in the story, this scene was enough to ban the film in Germany.**

In the world of child stars, Shirley was unique. Not only was she born with raw talent that was allowed to flourish under the watchful eye of her mother and her studio, but her timing was perfect in the progress of motion picture technology. Shirley was born the year after sound films (known as the

***Bright Eyes* confrontation: Shirley, Jane Withers and "Terry," the Cairn terrier who would achieve immortality as Toto in *The Wizard of Oz* five years later.**

"talkies") were successfully released to theaters. Child stars of the silent film era achieved a certain level of fame, but with a difference. While they were talented, attractive and well able to evoke audience reaction, their acting was exaggerated in an effort to compensate for a lack of verbal expression. Adding to the soap opera–like dramatics, typical storylines placed their characters in perilous or melodramatic situations to arouse audience sympathy. On screen, stars such as Jackie Coogan became flickering icons of an idealistic representation of childhood, distanced from the public without the benefit of sound. When the *Our Gang* shorts were filmed as "talkies," child actors were finally presented as real kids. Their directors were careful to pick up not only their rehearsed lines, but their intimate, offhand asides and chattering as well, adding to the charm and naturalness of the series. Another factor in *Our Gang's* appeal was the lack of heavy, doll-like makeup used for early studio lighting. As this technology improved, child actors lost the unreal quality of the past in favor of a fresh-faced look with a minimum of makeup.

While silent-era child stars had the ability to sing and dance, it was impossible to showcase them without a personal appearance. By the time sound was perfected, there were few kids on screen who were seasoned, all-around entertainers—those children were busy on the stages of the vaudeville circuit. If they happened to be filmed, their delivery was more in line with an adult belting a tune to the back of a packed house.

All these factors were in line when Shirley made her screen debut. Even as a toddler, she spoke clearly and distinctly, thanks to her mother's disdain for condescending baby talk. Shirley's singing voice was unforced and expressive—a perfect complement to the intricate dance steps that seemed effortless for her. Visually, her trademark blonde curls glowed while framing a face that took the light beautifully at any angle—it was as difficult to take one's eyes off Shirley on the screen as it was to get an unflattering shot of her on film. Talent, speech and charisma combined with the technology to present her to the public, contributing as much to Shirley's popularity as Shirley's ability itself.

*Bright Eyes* was released for Christmas, 1934. Shirley's second breakthrough, it finally determined a successful storyline for most of her later films. Written by director David Butler, who would guide Shirley through four of her best childhood features, the basic formula for a Temple film was set: Shirley was lacking either one or both parents. If she was an orphan, she had an adult family member or friend who adored and watched over her. She also had a protagonist who she would have to overcome. She usually lacked money, which mattered little to her. After resolving the problems of those around her, including finding a love interest for her guardian or single parent, she was rewarded at the end of the story with adoption and the promise of a comfortable life. Of course, to highlight her singing and dancing talent, there was a musical number as part of the plot—or two, or three.

*Bright Eyes* presented Shirley as the daughter of a pilot killed in an airplane crash whose housemaid mother is hit by a car on Christmas Eve. Her father's best friend (her Fox co-star James Dunn) adores her. She lives in an Art Deco mansion with the social-climbing Smythe family, who employed her late mother. The Smythes' wealthy Uncle Ned also adores her, but his family is dysfunctional to the core. They barely tolerate cohabitating with their curmudgeonly uncle in anticipation of his hefty estate and completely despise "the maid's child," as does their bratty daughter Joy (Jane Withers, a brilliant foil for Shirley). After all is said and done, Shirley stands up to Joy's abuse, reunites Dunn with his ex-sweetheart, helps him through a crash landing in a storm, sings "On The Good Ship Lollipop" (a tribute to an airplane, not a boat) and is finally adopted by Dunn and his new wife. They all move in with Uncle Ned, who banishes the hellish Smythes from his mansion, leaving them penniless. For her collective obnoxiousness, Joy's frustrated mother delivers a sound slap at the film's end. Pure satisfaction for a country in the midst of the Depression!

**Reserved seats for Shirley and co-star Jane Withers on the set of *Bright Eyes,* courtesy of director David Butler.**

After *Bright Eyes,* Shirley began a schedule of one film per quarter that would continue over the next two years. With Butler's direction, she made the children's classic *The Little Colonel* with Lionel Barrymore, a smash hit that paired her for the first time with the legendary tap dancer Bill "Bojangles" Robinson, and with Hattie McDaniel four years before her triumph as Mammy in *Gone With The Wind.* Other features included *Our Little Girl, Curly Top* (in which Shirley sang her other childhood standard "Animal Crackers in My Soup") and *The Littlest Rebel,* the first Shirley film released after Fox merged with 20th Century Films. After the major success of *The Little Colonel,* Shirley's place in Hollywood was assured. Her star began to rise in the box office ranking until she reached number one in 1935, surpassing the greats of Hollywood such as Clark Gable, Garbo and Mae West. She was honored by preserving her hand and footprints for posterity in the forecourt of Grauman's Chinese Theatre, and was awarded a special miniature Academy Award for her "outstanding contribution to the screen" in 1934. Audiences lined up for blocks in major markets to see her films. Her films were released in foreign countries, where she quickly became as popular as she was in the States. Her curls, dimples and smile were instantly

**Happy at home in *The Little Colonel:* Evelyn Venable, Hattie McDaniel and Shirley.**

recognizable; Fox's "overnight sensation" was literally everywhere. President Franklin Roosevelt publicly cited Shirley for raising the spirit of the nation with her film work, and gifted her with a specially inscribed photograph. The news media dubbed her the "Wonder Tot." She became the most photographed, most watched, most admired personality in the world.

Shirley, beyond it all, was both a complex and everyday seven-year-old.

The Temples carried on with what was now their usual schedule: Mr. Temple continued to work at the bank, her brothers attended school and Mrs. Temple accompanied Shirley back and forth to the studio. The only drastic change was a housekeeper. Shirley and her mother rehearsed her lines and delivery at bedtime while Mrs. Temple curled her hair, and Shirley would verbally enact the day's scene at breakfast. With a clear mind and sharp memory, Shirley was able to soak up her lines and those of the rest of the cast, mentally discarding them after the scene was through. She was able to repeatedly hit her marks on the set by the feel of the lighting on her face. Called "One–Take Temple" in the press, she did flub her lines every now and then. Newsreel outtakes for the Academy Awards ceremony in 1935 show two different takes of the supposedly spontaneous query "Mommy, can I go home now?" At one point, Shirley stumbles over the line with a self-critical "Ohh." It was late and she looked tired—major event or not, she probably was ready to sprint for the car. Her mom, sympathetic and smiling, apologizes: "She kinda bluffed it." The exchange is very revealing—there's no trace of admonishing or humiliation.

**Shirley not only received a special Academy Award in 1935, she also presented the Best Actress Oscar to Claudette Colbert for *It Happened One Night*. Shirley spent most of the long, late evening at her seat, shooting small pellets of bread across the table.**

The fact that Shirley could accomplish her job with the frenzied swirl of studio activity around her is a tribute to her mother, directors and Shirley's own work ethic. "Shirley Temple stood all alone in the midst of a brilliantly lighted ballroom," Samuel W. Morris reported in an article syndicated in 1935. "It was the first set in the filming of *The Littlest Rebel* on one of the big sound stages of the 20th Century-Fox studio. The cameras and lights were concentrated on the diminutive star. But more than two hundred men, women and children stood silently and watched. Every one of the silent crowd had something directly to do with the perfection of the final few seconds in which Shirley Temple's face would flash and twinkle and go serious for the screens of scores of theaters." The article goes on to detail the gathered crowd: Mrs. Temple, director David Butler, Shirley's teacher, special hairdresser, play supervisor, maid,

**Opposite: Shirley's Easter bonnet for 1935. By this time, she had preserved her hand and footprints in the forecourt of Grauman's Chinese Theatre.**

wardrobe mistress and doctor. Film workers included two assistant directors, a script girl, dialog director and four cameramen.

"At a little portable switchboard sat S.C. Chapman, controlling the mixture of sound from Shirley, from the orchestra, from the off-scene actors, which eventually goes to make what you hear in the theater. It required four others to help him at various points on and off the stage, placing microphones and cables about the set . . ." The ever-widening circle encompassed electricians, grips, carpenters, wardrobe handlers, a still photographer and prop men ("napkins must lie in the same folds, the ice cream must not melt too much, and the candles in the great crystal chandelier must stand up straight and new despite the blazing heat of the nearby arcs that really furnish the light"). Rounding out the regular crew were two watchmen who barred the sound stage doors and two janitors "leaning on their brooms" for a total of 51 people—in addition to the crowd of extras around the perimeter of the set. Somehow, through all the pandemonium, Shirley was able to beam her attention on the two people that mattered most: her mother and director. "Sparkle, Shirley," Mrs. Temple would coach from the sidelines before the cameras rolled. It was the key phrase that followed Shirley throughout her childhood career, enabling her to focus on the scene at hand despite the visual distraction of the people around her. This at an age when most kids struggle with a role in the annual school play!

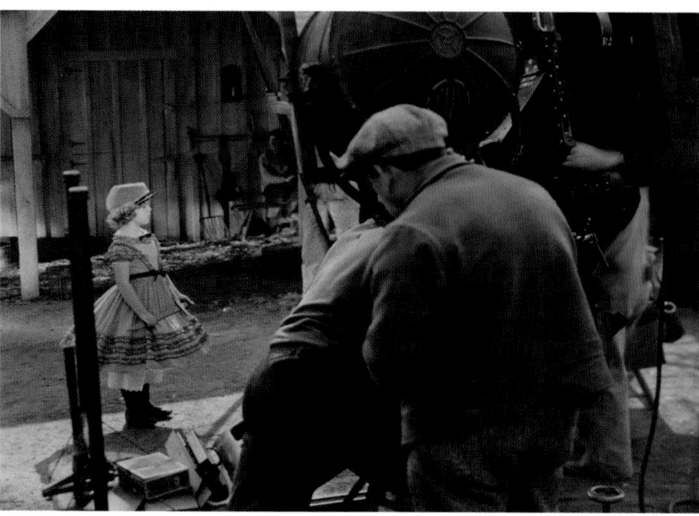

**Shirley focuses on her scene in *The Littlest Rebel* while director David Butler (in cap) looks on.**

**Opposite: An everyday sight at the Fox Studios–Mrs. Temple and her daughter arrive for work. Shirley, shown here in 1936, shields her eyes from the sun.**

Of course, there were times when other, more fascinating things caught Shirley's attention on the set (a game of "squares," a visitor, a practical joke on a cast member, inspecting the maze of equipment around her). It was up to Mrs. Temple to pull her daughter aside and firmly coax Shirley back to reality, long enough to do her job. Sometimes barter was involved—a promise of a cherished Coca-Cola from the crew's cooler after a scene was shot. Never was there a threat or ultimatum. Testing the limits of her director or mother was fun to a point, but Shirley innately understood the importance of what she did in relation to the rest of the team. If she held up production, she held up the film and therefore, the jobs of her buddies.

Sometimes, she was just tuckered out. "Shirley gets tired. What little girl wouldn't?" commented long-time Fox still photographer Anthony Ugrin in 1936. "On *Captain January,* waiting for a tedious 'setup' to be finished, the sandman got to her. It so happened I was shooting a 'grab shot' of her, but just as I clicked the shutter, she yawned. The result is one of the . . . most natural and real-kid pictures of Shirley I ever secured."

After a scene was completed it was reenacted for the still cameraman. Posing for stills was essentially the same as shooting live, except the lighting was rearranged and the actors went through the motions of each segment, holding their poses for a large format film camera. Still cameramen, such as Ugrin, were Shirley's pals and tried their best to expedite shooting stills to keep boredom from closing in. Ugrin was also responsible for off-guard, or candid shots of Shirley between scenes. Shirley would usually comply, but sometimes balked. "When I was ready to snap her, she'd run out of focus and hide. It was a game with her, but her unconscious rebellion put me on the spot because I had to produce pictures of her—or else . . . Between takes on the movie was playtime for her, and I got in the way." Ugrin empathized with Shirley and went on to describe the deal he made with his star: he would make a candid photo in one shot, then leave her alone if she wanted. He allowed Shirley to set his limit. "She never forgot it. When I set up my camera, she grins and holds up one finger. It's our code—'*one* shot!'"

**One of the countless Cinderella Brand Shirley Temple Frocks produced by Rosenau Brothers of Philadelphia.**

More taxing on Shirley was the endless parade of photographs for the Shirley Temple clothing line produced throughout her childhood. Mrs. Temple insisted that Shirley try on all the designs sold under her daughter's name as a method of quality control and truth in advertising. Three or four poses were taken of each dress, hat, scarf, coat, swimsuit, robe or pair of gloves to ensure one spectacular, signature shot to be used on a hang tag or in an ad. Holding these pretty, staged poses long enough to expose each sheet of film was difficult for a lively child (how many kids enjoy having a formal portrait taken?), but the process was complicated by a stylist standing nearby with the next dress ready to step into. The back seam was removed to spare the strain on Shirley's curls—any stray hair meant another restyling and time wasted. When the dust settled, Shirley would have posed for more than 20 product shots every few days at the height of her career. In retrospect, it's evident that she's just holding on until the last shot in some of the photographs. "It was just awful," Shirley Temple Black told a friend years later. "And [they] always came at the wrong time."

**Opposite: Shirley models an authentic Shirley Temple hat sold by Lewis & Son, New York. She was rarely photographed in profile.**

Posing for the great photographers of Hollywood, however, was just another day on the job with another colleague. George Hurrell recalled a relaxed Shirley falling asleep on a portrait set for *Wee Willie*

*Winkie* and taking the shot before she awoke. Another portrait shoot for *Heidi* was set against a huge floral arrangement. Hurrell posed and reposed Shirley to no avail. Unsatisfied with any result, he suddenly heard an invisible voice, hidden behind the immense vase. "Don't you think this would be best?" Shirley called out wearily. "Then you wouldn't have hardly any trouble at all."

Shirley herself was interested in making home movies, but unlike other stars, didn't enjoy being the subject. Pioneering cameraman Arthur Miller commented in *Filmo Topics,* in 1938, "When she isn't doing her stuff in [a] picture, and you aim a home-movie camera at her . . . she is just like any other eight-year-old. Conscious of the camera and having nothing definite to do, Shirley stiffens up; instead of the sweet youngster she really is, she becomes a self-conscious little girl. So my best shots of her were made during rehearsals for picture scenes or stolen with a telephoto lens when she didn't know anyone was filming her."

She was now making $2500 a week, a highly publicized sum in the mid-1930s, adding to the media's depiction of Hollywood royalty. "I'm glad I'm in the movies on account of I have so much money, 'specially since I got to be a star," Shirley supposedly told writer Jennie Lee. "I guess I have more money than anybody in the world." Far from flaunting it, Shirley viewed her salary as a form of fair barter for her hard work but only saw a modest allowance every week like any other child. The studio, however, was careful to inform the press that Shirley's earnings were being wisely invested for her future.

Her film earnings were greatly supplemented by royalties paid by companies licensing Shirley's name and image, creating a sub-industry centered around her. "Besides the people employed at the studio in Shirley's pictures, there are hundreds of other people who enjoy a salary each week on account of this child . . . her influence is felt all around the world," declared Franc Dillon in the dramatically titled article *Shirley Temple: Saver of Lives* in *Modern Screen* magazine. "There are the people that manufacture the Shirley Temple books, the Shirley Temple dresses [and] the Shirley Temple dolls, which must be manufactured, dressed and distributed." Shirley was creating jobs and in the case of piecework sewing for doll costumes, a cottage industry. This account doesn't include the profits made by those who used her image without authorization (before they were tracked down by lawyers for the Temples and Fox). Therefore, she was a true Depression-era heroine.

**Legendary photographer George Hurrell prepares to snap Shirley for a 1938 *Photoplay Magazine* color cover photo.**

Despite fame and fortune, the Temples attempted to keep Shirley centered in a neighborhood atmosphere. At the end of 1934, they moved from the small stucco

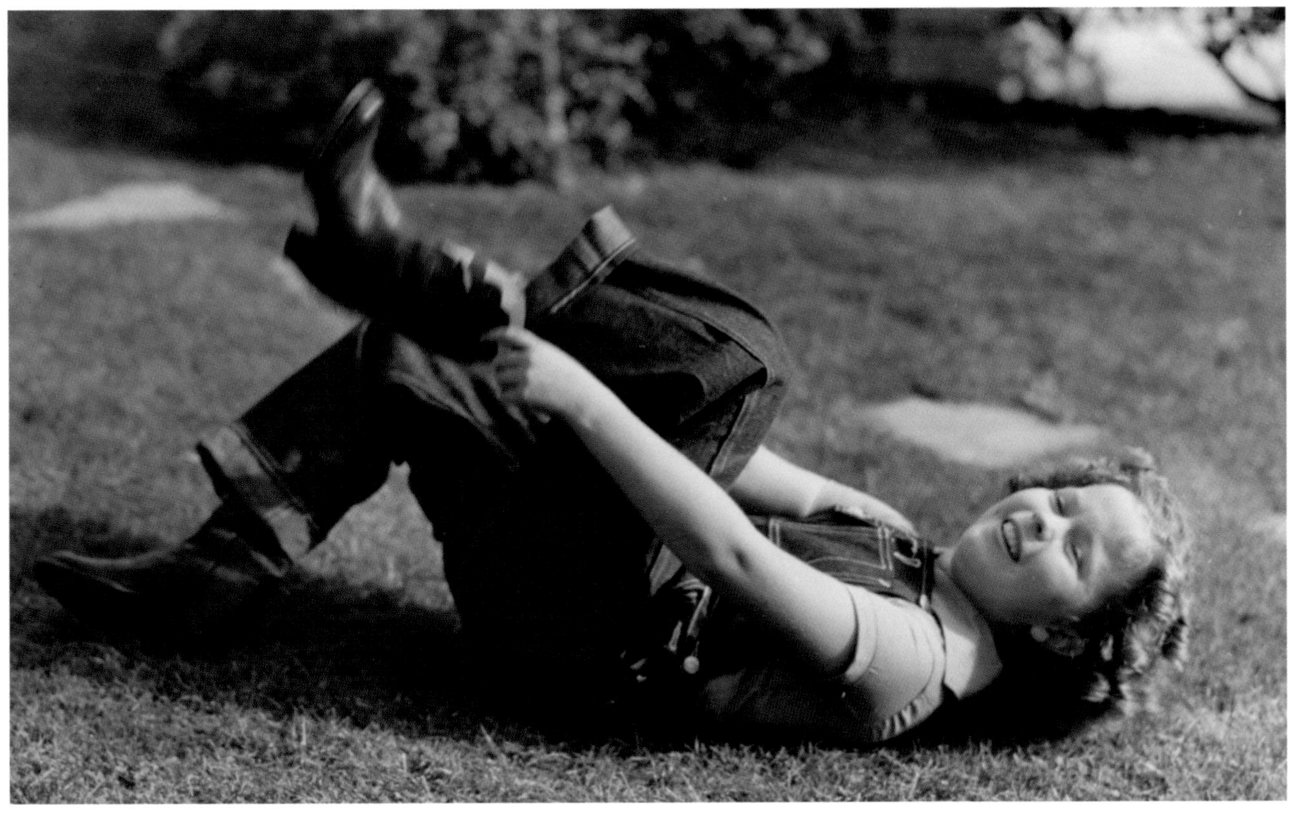

Shirley, togged for a romp on the lawn, pulls on a pair of prized cowboy boots. Overalls, jeans and playsuits were Shirley's clothing of choice when relaxing at home. Below: A bandana-ed Shirley keeps her hand on a toy six-shooter in a leather holster for a family snapshot.

bungalow where she was born to a larger home on a wide street in Santa Monica. It was impossible to keep the public away from her. Shirley and Mrs. Temple were trailed wherever they went—Mrs. Temple would later recall that an overzealous fan snipped off one of Shirley's curls in a crowded Los Angeles department store, terrifying her. Shopping excursions and beloved trips to the beach were over. Instead, Shirley played with her friends in a cheery Spanish style courtyard behind the house. The kids she interacted with knew her most of their lives and never mentioned the movie business. Work stayed at work until it was time to go over the script. Shirley, nowhere near the perceived image of a little girl in ruffly, fussy dresses, wore simple, tailored overalls and play frocks off the set and often wore her hair in curlers or under a bandana in private. She was an active "tomboy" who rode bicycles and horses, climbed trees and rolled around the lawn with her pet dogs. "My tastes were strictly blood and thunder," recalled teenage Shirley in her first official autobiography, *My Young Life,* published in 1945. She much preferred a stash of toy guns over the fabulous dolls being sent to her as gifts, and listened to *Gangbusters, Orphan Annie* and *The Shadow* on the radio. She wanted nothing more than to be a G-Man (the era's equivalent of today's federal agent) like her good

friend, FBI director J. Edgar Hoover. She loved games, a good practical joke as well as corny jokes, and informal people with a sense of humor. She enjoyed drawing, painting and writing. She hated to be manhandled by some visitors and fans who felt compelled to hug and kiss her, as if she were a possession.

Magazines and news syndicates clamored for exclusive interviews with Mrs. Temple, trying to tap into her secrets for the care and feeding of a child prodigy, to outline Shirley's eating habits, her height and weight, whether she was being overworked, her childhood illnesses, how often her hair was washed (once every two weeks), how many curls she had (the number varied between 55 and 56), or to relate Shirley's entire life story for the hundredth time. A doctored birth record was printed over and over to "prove" she was born in 1929 (when a 1936 fan newspaper printed the actual unretouched 1928 county birth certificate, the revelation quickly and quietly disappeared. The public—as well as Shirley—wouldn't discover her true age until she turned 13). Magazine sections ran lavish spreads showing Shirley's wardrobe, daily activities and home. "Personal" diary articles were printed, culling information from publicity releases and presenting Shirley's film work as "play"—along with an endless round of parties and events at which Shirley was the honored guest or hostess. Mainly, the public wanted to know how Shirley stayed so—*normal.*

**Opposite: Shirley took her correspondence with the overseas press seriously. Here, she composes a letter to *Cinegraf,* a Spanish-language movie magazine, in 1935.**

Press interviews were a part of Shirley's life since her early days in films. To prevent the negative effects of too many doting or prying reporters, Mrs. Temple would explain to Shirley that people wanted to know about her since she made them happy. For the most part, Shirley would be polite and accessible, except when she was tired or hungry. She was never prompted or coached in her replies: "I *guess* you're nice," decided Shirley, sizing up writer Neil Barclay, who was on assignment for *Screen Book* magazine in 1934. "To my intense relief, Shirley's mother didn't chide [her] for the words or the way she said them," Barclay continued. "Maybe that helps to explain Shirley. She is allowed thoughts about people, opinions distinctly her own . . ." Members of the overseas press also wanted to report back about the state of Shirley's health, growth or her working environment (a newspaper in England declared that Shirley was 30 years old and a midget; a European source claimed that all her hair had fallen out due to stress). Many reporters came to check out Mrs. Temple herself—a 1936 Fox in-house memo outlined a form of spin control when a faction of the media began to rumble that Shirley was being overworked and exploited by her mother. Shortly after this report, a large percentage of publicity photos presented Shirley greeting reporters and other visitors, interacting with the studio crew, and documenting her playtime between films to prove that she was indeed a normal, healthy child. The best childhood interview, however, came

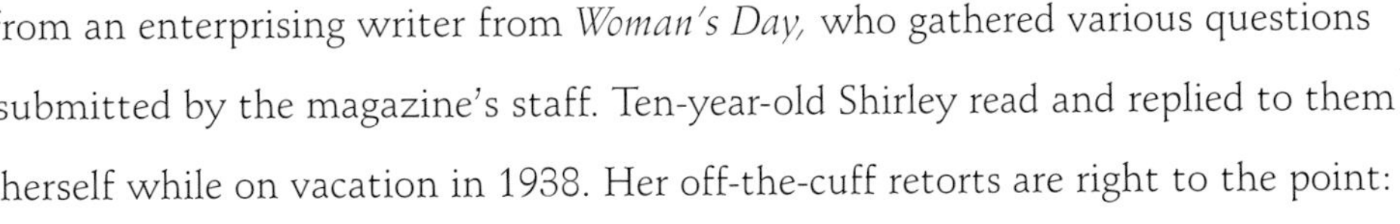

from an enterprising writer from *Woman's Day,* who gathered various questions submitted by the magazine's staff. Ten-year-old Shirley read and replied to them herself while on vacation in 1938. Her off-the-cuff retorts are right to the point:

> "Do you like dolls, or not? What do they mean, or not? . . . Can you ride horseback? Swim? Ski? Ride a bike? Not all at once. I can do everything but ski . . . Which picture was the most interesting for you to make—perhaps *Heidi?* Why do they ask the questions and answer them too? I liked all of them . . . Do you love to get home from your work—to your father, mother and all your playthings? What do they think, Mom—that you send me out to work and wait for me to come home? Don't they know you're with me wherever I go? . . . How do you feel about your brothers? That's silly! How do you feel about YOUR brothers?"

When more and more sightseers with the aid of Hollywood maps turned up on their Santa Monica lawn, the Temples built a private estate on Rockingham Road in Brentwood, on a hillside with a distant view of the ocean. Here Shirley could relax, play, ride her horses, bicker with her brothers or learn to swim in the pool without being interrupted. The Normandy-style house had a large playroom for Shirley and was surrounded by a fence that was equipped with a massive "electric gate" to prevent unwanted visits. The gate got as much publicity as Shirley's new home during an era when kidnapping was a real threat. The Temple family received quite a few directed at Shirley—notably one Nebraska teen who demanded a hefty payoff not to abduct her, and another gentleman who publicly claimed Shirley was his daughter. Nonetheless, Shirley would make occasional appearances at the gate for fans' cameras with her pal "Grif" by her side.

John Griffith arrived as Shirley's bodyguard when Fox merged with 20th Century Pictures in 1935. A childhood pal of new studio head Darryl Zanuck, Grif saved Zanuck from drowning when both were young. In repayment, Zanuck promoted Grif and his wife Mabel to the roles of Shirley's bodyguard and personal maid. A great team, Grif and Mabel looked after Shirley as much as the Temple family did, and had an interactive role in the household. Tall, handsome and strapping, Grif was energetic enough to keep up with Shirley, who enjoyed teasing him by sprinting out of his sight whenever possible. He was

**Opposite: Shirley keeps her coif in place with curlers while staying astride her bucking pony. Powerful Grif holds the pony's front legs to keep Shirley from flying off in another direction (though she probably would have enjoyed it)!**

**Left: Grif would often be found running behind Shirley while she rode her bike; and a gag shot showed that Shirley was "strong" enough to push her bodyguard into the pool. Below: Grif's wife Mabel poses with Shirley's favorite pet—her Pekinese puppy, Ching-Ching (or "Chingie").**

First home in Santa Monica.

Shirley entertains a pal in the courtyard of her second home (Mrs. Temple stands by).

Second home in Santa Monica, circa 1935.

Shirley's very Hollywood dressing table in her studio bungalow. Her school desk is reflected in the mirror.

The Brentwood estate, circa 1937.

Bungalow dressing room on the Fox lot, given to Shirley for privacy at the studio.

Playroom at the Brentwood estate (designed by Howard Verbeck).

As Shirley's career progressed, the Temples moved from the simple Santa Monica bungalow where Shirley was born to a larger home with an enclosed courtyard on a quiet street several blocks away. Shirley's status as American royalty soon required a more private dwelling befitting a cinema princess, so the Temples built a charming home (designed by John Byers) on an estate in the exclusive Brentwood area. Both J. Edgar Hoover and John Griffith took credit for installing the security equipment, including a massive gate (opposite) that would swing open for announced visitors. Shirley would sometimes make an appearance there (with Grif in tow) to the delight of tourists with cameras. For peace, quiet and privacy at the Fox studio, Shirley was given a bungalow with child-sized furniture. Shirley's home and bungalow fascinated Depression-era audiences; both were featured in magazines such as *Architectural Digest* and *House Beautiful*. Below: A pen-and-ink drawing by a fan of the 1930s.

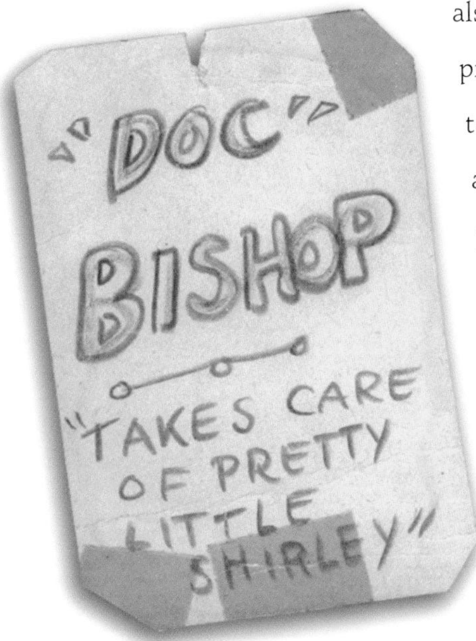


also sport enough to take Shirley's practical jokes, but his background presence was comforting enough to finally give the Temples the freedom to take Shirley on short breaks to Palm Springs, or to drive her to Vancouver or across the country with little fear. He was armed, and this fascinated his young client. Scrapbooks kept by Mabel and Grif over the years show that there was real affection in their relationship with Shirley: personal snapshots, artwork and Valentines were preserved within their pages. Grif and Mabel stayed with Shirley until the end of her Fox career.

Since relationships with her costars were fleeting, the steady crew that supported Shirley became her closest friends. She was just Shirley or "Pruney;" in turn, she had nicknames for most of them. Wendell "Doc" Bishop handled her publicity, Harry Brand took care of studio affairs, Frances Klampt ("Klammie") was her studio teacher, "Jonesy" was the propmaster, lifelong friend Mary Lou Isleib was her stand-in, Waldo Ahlstrom took care of the ever-growing menagerie at the Temple estate—and beloved "Uncle Billy" Robinson was her greatest dancing partner and mentor. Uncle Billy adored Shirley, whom he called "the greatest tap dancer for her age in the world." He would coach her in their numbers and Shirley would learn simply by listening to the sound of his feet. Neither Shirley nor her parents perceived racial barriers in an age when the dancing duo's holding hands on screen was deleted in certain areas of the country. When Uncle Billy visited her on vacation in Palm Springs, she was puzzled as to why he was staying in the segregated chauffeurs' quarters, rather than in the main building. "I'm staying with *my* chauffeur," Uncle Billy explained with a grin. Photos of the pair together show genuine affection.

Friends in her peer group were also few, but prized. As Shirley's career progressed, she had less time for socializing beyond her studio responsibilities, and was kept separate from the other child players in her films due to her required study breaks with Klammie. She did play with local children when she vacationed in Palm Springs and Hawaii. They had known Shirley for years, ignored her fame and didn't stand around uncomfortably gaping at her. Existing newsreel outtakes from one Palm Springs break show an easy interaction with her buddies and no aloofness at all on Shirley's part. Much was made of the fact that even though her public appearances were carefully monitored and few, Shirley wasn't kept behind glass as a breakable object; she projected an air of accessibility. One outstanding article from this era was Ida Zeitlin's

**Shirley's publicity agent, Doc Bishop, acted as press protector, buddy, and often personal assistant. His job was not only to garner media exposure for his star, but to make sure she was content on the set and off—which often meant that he would find himself involved in a game of "Squares," or acting as Deputy to Shirley's Texas Ranger (opposite). The occupational ID tag, above left, was probably given to Doc at a studio party. Below: Waldo Ahlstrom took care of Shirley's pets, including her pony, "Spunky."**

With Bill Robinson in a posed stair dance for *The Little Colonel* (1935).

With George Murphy in *Little Miss Broadway* (1938).

With Charlotte Greenwood and Jack Oakie in *Young People* (1940).

Showing off their "taps": Shirley and her beloved Uncle Billy "Bojangles" Robinson in 1937 (opposite). Bojangles appeared with Shirley for the first time in *The Little Colonel* (1935), in which the pair performed a famous dance routine on a plantation mansion staircase. He would go on to star with Shirley in three other features, and choreographed the dances for *Dimples* (1936). Lifelong friends, Bojangles presented Shirley with several elaborate gifts, including every kid's fantasy—a real, gas-powered automobile that Shirley would pilot around the lot (with a speed regulator). Shirley had several notable dancing partners during her career, and matched steps with all of them. Below: Shirley rehearses the intricate, nerve tap routine for the finale of *The Poor Little Rich Girl* (1936).

With Buddy Ebsen, rehearsing "The Codfish Crawl" for *Captain January* (1936).

"Ginger Rogers and Fred Astaire" in *Stowaway* (1936).

With Jack Haley and Alice Faye in *The Poor Little Rich Girl* (1936).

With Jimmy Durante in a scene cut from *Little Miss Broadway* (1938).

Minstrel show finale with the Hall Johnson Choir *for Dimples* (1936).

**Frances Klampt, Shirley's private teacher at the Fox studio, was known by the nickname her famous student gave her: "Klammie."**

**Opposite: Schoolwork can sometimes be a drag–Shirley takes a study break during the filming of *Captain January*. Inset: two examples of Shirley's homework assignments: addition, subtraction and "Danger! Men at Work."**

*If Shirley Temple Came to Your Home,* from a 1939 issue of *Movie Mirror.* Pure fantasy, it presented the scenario of Shirley visiting a normal family on a random day: "'Hello,' says Shirley, sticking out a friendly paw. 'I'm Shirley Temple.' [She was] under the mistaken necessity of identifying herself." The story goes on to imagine the interaction of Shirley with the entranced 13-year-old daughter of the family and the pre-visit reaction of the totally unimpressed 11-year-old son: "He howls at having his Saturday afternoon ball game interfered with . . . 'What am I s'posed to do? Play Ring Around the Rosy with her?' he mutters. He waxes ironic in falsetto: 'Hello Shirley. Howja do, Shirley? You're lookin' elegant, Shirley. You were wonderful in your picture, Shirley, even if I didn't get to see it, cause I'd rather see a wild Western any day, so put *that* in your little pipe and smoke it!'"

As Shirley became famous, more and more celebrated visitors sought her out to bask in her glory—Eleanor Roosevelt used her as a subject for her daily column *My Day;* Amelia Earhart gifted her with a matched set of airline luggage; Noel Coward empathized with Shirley's frustration with fractions; J. Edgar Hoover arrived with a Minox spy camera "just like the G-Men use." Most came to meet the most famous child in the world while others came solely to be photographed with her to gain publicity for themselves. Several were foreign visitors—including delegates and royalty from other countries. Some visitors brought their children: Helen Hayes' daughter Mary McArthur inspected Shirley's dollhouse; actress Joan Davis' four-year-old daughter Beverly boasted that she was Shirley's "personal comedian"; Irving Berlin's daughter Mary Ellin watched Shirley rehearse a scene in *Heidi.* To keep Shirley's head from spinning, teacher Klammie designed lesson plans to coincide with the day's callers, transferring Shirley's sense of importance to theirs.

**Shirley and four-year-old admirer Beverly Davis on the set of *Rebecca of Sunnybrook Farm.***

Shirley learned about the country and occupation of each admirer. For her part, Shirley greeted all with an air of hospitality in the special bungalow that Fox gave her as an oasis from the distracting setting of the studio commissary. Shirley's bungalow was equipped with an old-fashioned cast iron school desk so she could study with Klammie for the required two hours a day away from the set. With her teacher's close attention and creative lessons, Shirley was able to advance easily through the requisite Los Angeles

November 13, 1936

2
62
83
47
+39
231

1
61
93
26
+19
199

2
71
58
8
+76
213

1
62
15
76
+84
237

2
28
29
+93
150

1
48
63
+67
178

69
93
+14
166

97
29
+78
204

76
-45
31

59
-20
39

108
-65
43

68
-32
36

98
-61
37

61
-20
41

147
-87
60

84
-31
53

75
-48
37

49
-9
40

29
-6
23

47
-20
27

Danger!

Men at Work

I saw lots of men working on the street this morning. They had big shovels and were digging up the street.

Shirley Temple.

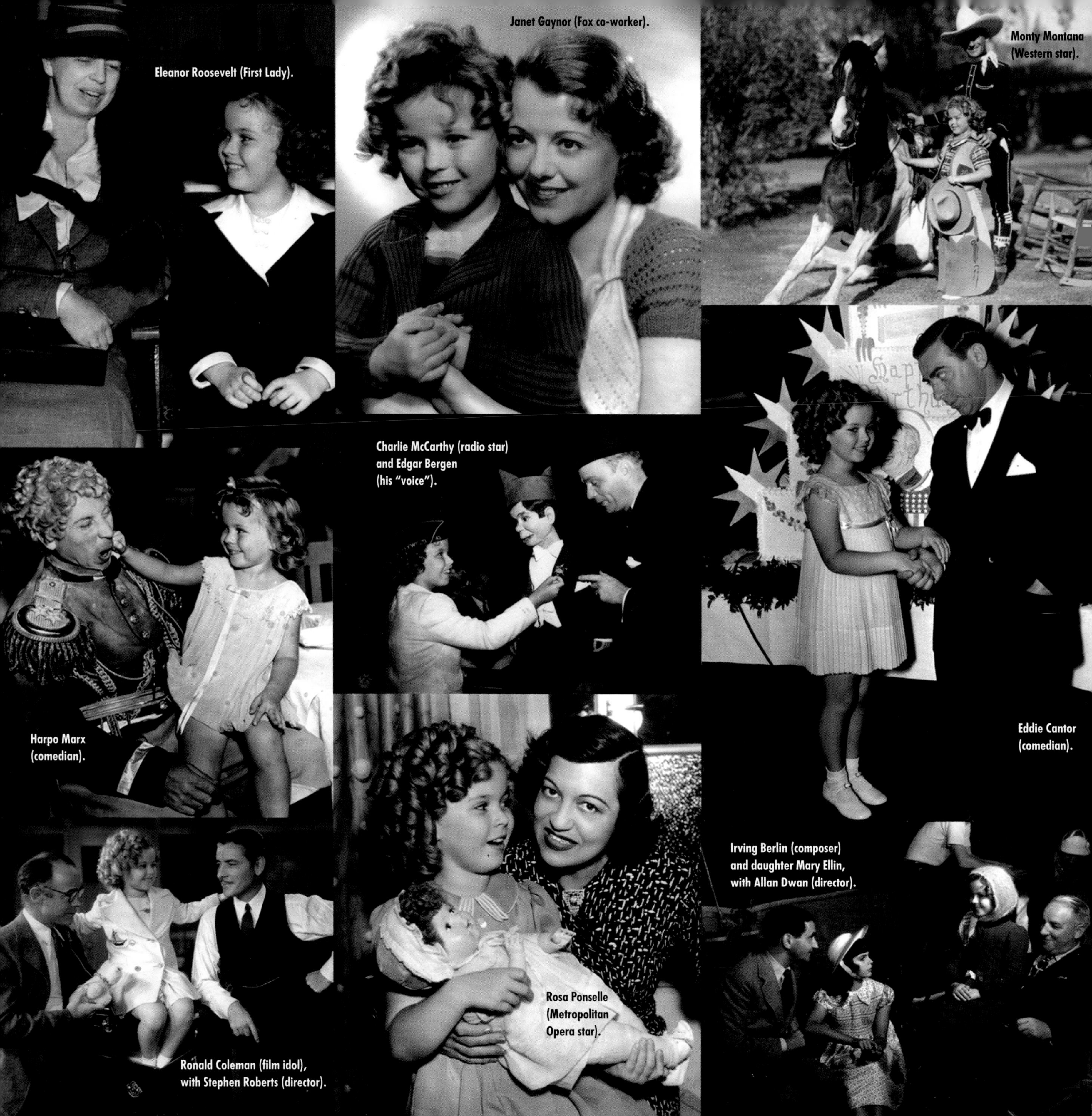

Eleanor Roosevelt (First Lady).

Janet Gaynor (Fox co-worker).

Monty Montana (Western star).

Charlie McCarthy (radio star) and Edgar Bergen (his "voice").

Eddie Cantor (comedian).

Harpo Marx (comedian).

Rosa Ponselle (Metropolitan Opera star).

Irving Berlin (composer) and daughter Mary Ellin, with Allan Dwan (director).

Ronald Coleman (film idol), with Stephen Roberts (director).

J·C·
Shirley dear:
Happy Birthday
and love
Joan Crawford

What could make Joan Crawford so jittery as to run out of the house without her pumps? Meeting Shirley Temple, her "favorite star," for the first time on the set of *Little Miss Broadway* in April of 1938. "Say, I'm so nervous I'm sick at my stomach!" Joan reportedly told Hollywood columnist Cal York, on hand to take notes while the two mega-stars visited. Joan watched Shirley rehearse an intricate dance number, then presented her with a box of candy for her upcoming birthday. The gift card was later given to Shirley's bodyguard, and is presented below.

A uniform, thundering horses, a location shoot in the hills of California—all priceless for *Wee Willie Winkie's* leading lady.

school board tests issued to monitor her progress. Shirley's homework, photographed just as she wrote it, held fascination for her fans.

After studio head Darryl Zanuck's arrival as part of the Fox Films–20th Century merger, Shirley's films became more elaborate, with more costume or "period" films and several remakes of childhood classics. Zanuck was convinced that Shirley, far from being a typical child star with a short-lived career, would "last forever" if her stories were carefully chosen as she grew. Although they were always first class features, production quality increased and musical numbers became more intricate. *The Littlest Rebel,* set at the start of the Civil War, showcased Shirley and Bill Robinson in two sophisticated tap sequences (and Shirley's character pleading with Abraham Lincoln to pardon her Confederate officer father). *Captain January* featured Shirley swooping over barrels and docks with twice-her-height Buddy Ebsen, and a tricky tap dancing solo down a spiral staircase as she recited multiplication tables. *The Poor Little Rich Girl* teamed Shirley with veterans Jack Haley and Alice Faye in an intense, carefully timed military tap number, an amazing accomplishment for an eight-year-old child. *Dimples* had Shirley as the head of a genuine minstrel show (and playing "Little Eva" in *Uncle Tom's Cabin*). *Stowaway* displayed Shirley's talent at mimicking Eddie Cantor, Al Jolson and Ginger Rogers—with a child-sized dummy of Fred Astaire strapped to her shoes. *Heidi* had a fantasy minuet sequence and a clog dance with Shirley in a Dutch outfit, flying into the scene on a high wire, which thrilled her. But her favorite film of this period featured no dancing at all.

1937's *Wee Willie Winkie* was Shirley's first film since *Little Miss Marker* to rely solely on her dramatic acting ability. Retooled from Rudyard Kipling's original story, the character of "Winkie" became a girl, and allowed Shirley to wear the kilted uniform of the Seventh Highlanders. Shirley was thrilled with the garment, practiced her drills for the picture long after her workday was over and begged to be allowed to wear it home. Directed by John Ford (whom Shirley dubbed "Ford V-8"), she starred with Victor McLaglen and Cesar Romero, reforming the evil Khoda Khan at the famous Khyber Pass (filmed in Chatsworth, California). Her acting won kudos from most, especially the fact that she was able to carry a picture without the usual Temple formula. The film was given a classic Hollywood premiere complete with searchlights,

**Shirley took these mini-photos of pals Johnnie (Grif), Harry (Brand) and "Chick" with the Minox spy camera given to her by FBI Director J. Edgar Hoover. One of her subjects turned the camera on her for the last frame.**

**The original United Costumers-tagged cap carried by Shirley in *Wee Willie Winkie* (the one worn by her was specially made to fit around her curls).**

grandstands set up for the crowds, a special house that encased a display of Shirley's toys, and a larger-than-life statue of Shirley and McLaglen placed near the theater. Reviews were generally good, citing Shirley's maturing thespian talent without the aid of superfluous songs and dances. There was one notable dissenting voice from overseas—London novelist and critic Graham Greene purportedly reviewed *Winkie* in his short-lived magazine *Night and Day.* Instead, Greene devoted almost an entire column to what he described as Shirley's "dimpled depravity." Intimating that Shirley's childhood image was a thinly-disguised masquerade for the hidden desires of middle-aged men and clergymen, Greene commented " . . . her appeal is more secret and more adult . . . two years ago she was a fancy little piece. Now . . . she is a complete totsy." Greene's commentary included a suggestive critique of her film costumes and dancing; only ten lines were reserved for an indifferent review of the film. The controversial bit was effective, to a point—newsstand posters screamed "Sex and Shirley Temple" and the October 28, 1937 issue sold out. *Night and Day* filed for bankruptcy a short time later, due to several lawsuits filed against it for various matters—including one by the Temples and Fox.

**Opposite: One of Shirley's first real glamour portraits from 1937.**

Despite the claim that Shirley was actually a 30- or 40-year-old dwarf and/or a mother of four, there was no denying that she was growing up. Physical changes over the span of Shirley's career had been subtle for audiences used to seeing Shirley on the screen every few months. Unlike television reruns or videos, one didn't have a linear point of reference to track Shirley's growth as easily as viewers can today. By the time Shirley filmed *Rebecca of Sunnybrook Farm* in the late fall of 1937, it was clear she was maturing. No longer a cute "wonder tot," her appearance was starting to reflect the beauty of her adult years (several glamour portraits were made during this period). The head full of bouncy curls was no longer appropriate for a nine-and-a-half-year-old who was both worldly and mischievous. Mrs. Temple wisely opted for a simpler coiffure—Shirley's thick, wavy hair was tied into two curly ponytails, a change that was heralded both in the film and in the press. At this point, her hair was allowed to darken naturally to a deep strawberry blonde shade (those who saw Shirley on her well-publicized cross-country trip the following year were surprised to note that she appeared to be a redhead instead of the expected blonde!)

**The issue of Graham Greene's *Night and Day* containing the review of *Wee Willie Winkie* that caused a ruckus reaching from the United Kingdom to the United States.**

Shirley had already experienced a professional setback in her ninth year—losing the role of Dorothy in *The Wizard of Oz.* An avid fan of the *Oz* book series, Shirley had long wanted to "meet" Dorothy rather than play the role ("She's real," Shirley Temple Black remembered remarking to her mother in *Child Star*), but losing the role was still a disappointment. Added to this was a brief hospitalization for her mother that separated them for the first time in Shirley's life, and a slight downward trend in attendance at

Shirley and chauffeur Gus (Bert Lahr) play in a deluxe apartment house garage in ***Just Around the Corner*** **(1938).**

Shirley's films. Her audience base continued to be strong, however, and she remained the top box office draw in the world— a position she held since 1935. Zanuck began to line up big-budget projects that would reflect Shirley's growth and appeal to a wider audience. "We spent more money on *Wee Willie Winkie* than on any prior Temple picture," Zanuck announced in the June 14, 1937 issue of Fox's in-house publication, *The New Dynamo.* "We will continue spending that kind of money. We have very ambitious plans for [Shirley's] continued reign as queen of the screen."

1938's *Rebecca of Sunnybrook Farm,* a musical with no apparent similarity to the famous Kate Douglas Wiggins tale, was geared to kids and adults with songs that became popular hits, sophisticated humor and a jazz finale featuring Shirley singing and dancing to Raymond Scott's "The Toy Trumpet" with Bill Robinson. To emphasize the fact that Shirley was growing up, she sang a medley of familiar tunes from her early childhood. Her next film, *Little Miss Broadway,* boasted an all-star cast including future California Senator George Murphy, Jimmy Durante and a lineup of veteran entertainers. The finale featured Murphy and Shirley in an energetic dance routine over a fantasy New York City skyline. *Just Around the Corner* starred Shirley with Charles Farrell, Joan Davis and Bert Lahr in a screwball musical comedy that pitted Shirley against a madcap, upscale family that moves into her unemployed architect father's New York penthouse when he takes a job as the building superintendent. Shirley was paired with Bill Robinson for a final screen duet, gained a puppy-love interest in the son of the penthouse dwellers, and acted as the livewire tomboy she truly was ("You can't fool a G-Woman!" she bragged to neighborhood bullies in one scene). While these films hold up well today and are great fun, the stories basically stuck to the tried-and-true Shirley Temple formula and didn't attract audiences in droves as Zanuck had hoped.

**Opposite: 1938's *Rebecca of Sunnybrook Farm* contrasted the fast-paced world of radio shows with the simple life "down on the farm." Shirley's new ponytailed hairdo made front-page news when the film was released.**

Shirley continued to remain unspoiled, to the never-ending amazement of the press. Occasionally, she was presented as "fresh" or impudent, just like any kid who rebels against her elders. She still cried "Hi pals!" when she greeted the film crew, loved to play jokes and wisecrack with the cast. "How's the weather over there?" Shirley would yell to visitors who were watching her performance in awe from the sidelines. She had endless energy—it was hard for adult players to keep up with her. "Sakes alive, what a child!" enthused exhausted *Broadway* costar Edna Mae Oliver after watching Shirley execute an especially athletic dance routine. Miss Oliver, in contrast, had only two lines in the scene.

**The dream sequence from *The Little Princess* in which Shirley played a dual role: a regal princess complete with a court, and one of the troupe of ballet dancers who entertained her.**

One outlet for Shirley's energy, both physical and philanthropical, was the initiation of the Shirley Temple Police Force. Shirley began deputizing cast, crew and friends shortly after filming *Wee Willie Winkie,* using paper clips as badges. Shirley would review her troops daily—various dime, nickel and quarter fines were issued for infractions such as forgetting to wear one's clip to the set. Fines would then be used for donations to local children's charities. The Force was made official when a crew member had special brass-plated shields made for the cause. Shirley took her Police ranks seriously—badges were never to be traded off or passed out as souvenirs, and fines were collected regularly.

In a bid to change the course of Shirley's screenplays, Fox slated four major projects for 1939: *The Little Princess, Susannah of the Mounties, The Little Diplomat* and *Lady Jane.* The latter two were never made. *Lady Jane,* a mystery set in Victorian-era New Orleans (with the story's climax set at the Mardi Gras), seems the most intriguing of the four—its premise could have set Shirley's career in a new direction. Instead, 1939's *The Little Princess* was filmed as a lavish production in Technicolor; it was Shirley's first color film since a special ending sequence for *The Little Colonel* in 1935. The riches-to-rags-to-riches tale was based on Frances Hodgson Burnett's *Sara Crewe or What Happened at Miss Minchin's.* Shirley starred as a wealthy, pampered London boarding school student who is demoted to house servant when her Captain father is listed as missing during the Boer War. Shirley's character, banished to a cold garret room, appeared as an imaginary princess in a Maxfield Parrish-inspired dream sequence where she also danced ballet (although Shirley had some training, Mrs. Temple was careful not to allow her to dance on pointe without substantial experience). The story ends happily when Shirley is reunited with her wounded father in a hospital ward—with the help of Queen Victoria! The film was widely promoted by Zanuck as Shirley's best dramatic screen achievement and given another major Hollywood premiere. *Princess* did well at the time, and is still one of her best-remembered, most viewed films.

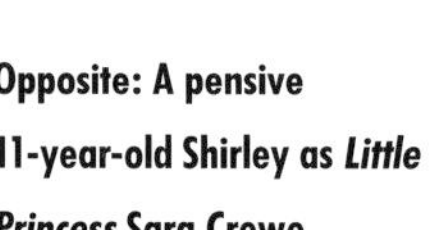

**Opposite: A pensive 11-year-old Shirley as *Little Princess* Sara Crewe.**

1939 showed that Shirley's box office status was slipping (she was displaced in the top spot by Mickey Rooney, and was now at number five in the top ten). Audiences still preferred escapist entertainment, but dynamic musicals featuring teenage entertainers such as Rooney, Judy Garland and Deanna Durbin were rapidly gaining popularity. However, Shirley continued to maintain the same level of fame and recognition she enjoyed for the previous four years. She was still followed wherever she and her family

SHIRLEY
TEMPLE
POLICE

"I want to be a G-Man," Shirley would firmly state when asked what she wanted to be when she grew up. Shirley was fascinated by radio programs such as *Gang Busters* and *The Shadow;* her favorite playthings were a stash of toy guns. Thus, the Shirley Temple Police Force was born – an exclusive fraternity that existed on Fox sound stages. Cast, crew and guests alike were presented with specially-made badges; fines were doled out by Chief Temple for unpolished or forgotten shields during a daily

inspection of her squad. Proceeds were then donated to charity. This gave Shirley, used to taking direction, an opportunity to assert control and live out her fantasy–culminated by the presentation of a badge to her pal J. Edgar Hoover, the Boss G-Man, himself. Other willing recipients were Native American child actor Martin Good Rider (top) and *Look* magazine editor Vernon Pope (right).

went, fans clamored for any scrap of a news bit or article, she was an icon all over the world—even though the war overseas was beginning to curtail film distribution from the States. Although some theater owners were submitting messages to trade publications such as "Sorry, but Shirley has lost all her appeal to my public," people were still in awe of Shirley and her accomplishments at such a young age.

*Susannah of the Mounties,* co-starring Shirley with Randolph Scott, followed to fair reviews. Members of the Blackfoot Indian tribe were transported to Hollywood to add authenticity to the movie, intriguing Shirley and giving her another screen boyfriend in Martin Good Rider. Next on the roster came Fox's answer to *The Wizard of Oz,* Maurice Maeterlinck's *The Blue Bird.* It was Shirley's last film of the decade. Although it was praised for state-of-the-art special effects, the big-budget effort was Shirley's first real box office failure. Like *Oz,* it was filmed in sepiatone and Technicolor; unlike *Oz,* the story relied on heavy symbolism that was too intense for a society on the verge of World War II. Shirley played a truly disagreeable child for the first time in her career as self-absorbed "Mytyl." She and her little brother "Tyltyl" (Johnny Russell) embark on a dream quest for the elusive Blue Bird of Happiness, accompanied by human equivalents of their lovable pet bulldog, their witch-like cat and guiding "Light" (a luminous, benevolent fairy). The soul-searching journey involved visiting their deceased grandparents in the Past, meeting their future sister in the Land of Unborn Children, experiencing excess in the Land of Luxury, and escaping a spectacular forest fire that kills their evil cat—only to awake and find that the Blue Bird was always alive and well in their own back yard. Despite a major promotion by Fox, "*The Blue Bird* laid an egg," Shirley herself would comment in later years.

**Opposite: Shirley, the sophisticated adolescent schoolgirl and star in 1939.**

1940's *Young People,* Shirley's last childhood film, reused the familiar Temple formula with a new twist. The story—a vaudeville family retires and moves to a New England farm—had a feeling similar to the popular *Andy Hardy* movies; "teenage" films produced at the time the term was being popularized, and precursors to the "family" television series of the 1950s. Besides singing and dancing to perfection with veterans Jack Oakie and Charlotte Greenwood, Shirley interacted with kids her own age and dealt with the universal problems of rejection, acceptance and recognition of growing up. In retrospect, it's interesting to think of the possibilities for Shirley's future films if the studio developed stories in this genre for her. Instead, Fox and the Temples mutually agreed to let the last 13 months of Shirley's contract lapse in May of

**Shirley as the ever-impatient Mytyl with Eddie Collins and Gayle Sondergaard (the human equivalents of sweet Tylo the bulldog and malicious Tylette the cat) in 1939's *The Blue Bird*.**

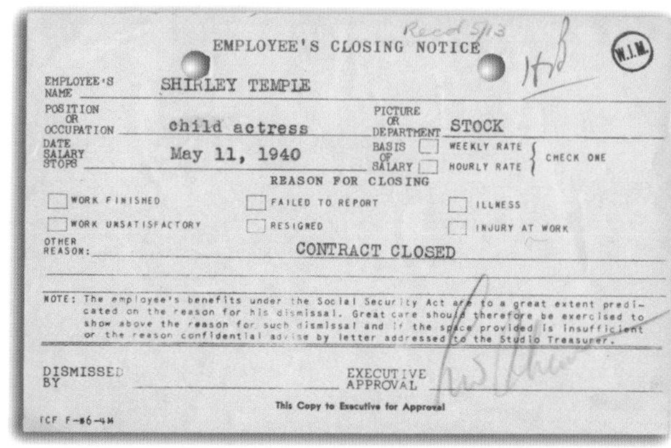

EMPLOYEE'S CLOSING NOTICE

EMPLOYEE'S NAME: SHIRLEY TEMPLE

POSITION OR OCCUPATION: child actress — PICTURE OR DEPARTMENT: STOCK

DATE SALARY STOPS: May 11, 1940 — BASIS OF SALARY: ☐ WEEKLY RATE ☐ HOURLY RATE (CHECK ONE)

REASON FOR CLOSING

☐ WORK FINISHED ☐ FAILED TO REPORT ☐ ILLNESS

☐ WORK UNSATISFACTORY ☐ RESIGNED ☐ INJURY AT WORK

OTHER REASON: CONTRACT CLOSED

NOTE: The employee's benefits under the Social Security Act are to a great extent predicated on the reason for his dismissal. Great care should therefore be exercised to show above the reason for such dismissal and if the space provided is insufficient or the reason confidential advise by letter addressed to the Studio Treasurer.

DISMISSED BY ______ EXECUTIVE APPROVAL ______

This Copy to Executive for Approval

TCF F-#6-4M

1940. Fox cited that they were unsure what to do with Shirley at the start of what was called the "awkward age"—the teen years—and the Temples maintained that Fox opted to repeatedly choose poor stories for her.

The public was reluctant to let her go. News of her retirement merited front-page placement alongside major war reports. Columnists speculated on the next phase of Shirley's career, even though she was settling into private life for the first time since she was three. "Why not a Disney animated picture with a single, real-life character—Shirley?" suggested columnist Jimmie Fidler, one of Shirley's lifelong supporters. "It could be a sort of *Alice in Wonderland* fantasy, with Miss Temple surrounded by all the odd little figures Walt's cartoonists can invent and bring to life."

Shirley was 12 years old when she officially retired, though the studio still stated that she was 11. She had an eight-year film career behind her—four years at the top of the box office and total earnings well in excess of three million dollars. She was a Kentucky Colonel, mascot of several international naval fleets, the Gold Star Child of Peace, an honorary Texas Ranger, the youngest Grand Marshal of the Tournament of Roses Parade, winner of countless awards and the youngest Academy Award honoree. She had fan clubs in almost every country on the globe, had a junior cocktail named for her and was recognized even in the remotest parts of the world. The famous and near-famous paid homage to her. She was an undeniable Hollywood legend. Most kids of her age were getting ready for Junior High.

Sensing a professional change on the horizon, Mrs. Temple enrolled Shirley at the private Westlake School for Girls in the fall of 1939, months before her retirement. She assimilated into seventh grade and became a Camp Fire Girl with the name "Keri-Woh-Sune-Anang" or "Bright Shining Star." She was still a normal kid, seemingly untouched by all the attention and the awareness of her fame. She had learned early about responsibility to a world audience: an outgrowth of this was the beginning of a public service career that continued into her adulthood. As a youngster she visited children's hospitals and made appearances and newsreel segments endorsing a new charity formed to fight polio—the March of Dimes. She acted as spokesperson in a short film for the American Red Cross. She helped to raise funds for the 1940 Olympic Games in Finland and addressed the 1939 *New York Herald Tribune* Forum by phone from Hollywood to comment on a special children's section at the upcoming World's Fair. She was involved with the American Legion and the Shriners, drawing attention to their humanitarian work simply by appearing at their events.

**A standard issue Twentieth Century-Fox employee closing notice gives Shirley's "retirement" date as May 11, 1940—ending her six-and-a-half year association with the studio. In that time, she spent four years as the number-one ranked box office star, and saved Fox from bankruptcy. Below: *Friday* magazine for June 7, 1940 announced Shirley's retirement with a headline worthy of royalty—"Shirley Abdicates."**

**Opposite: Shirley, about to enter her teenage years in 1940—the star of *Young People,* her final film for Fox.**

Restless with a day-to-day school schedule and used to the varied environment of the studio, Shirley re-entered the acting field at age 13. A contract with Metro-Goldwyn-Mayer included the proposal of starring with Mickey Rooney and Judy Garland in the upcoming musical *Broadway Melody of 1942.* The opportunity never materialized; instead Shirley made an adolescent drama, *Kathleen,* in 1941. Her "second" film career had begun and was basically scheduled around her school year at Westlake until her graduation in 1945. Shirley starred in David O. Selznick's classic WWII homefront story *Since You Went Away* (1943), the film version of Broadway's *Kiss and Tell* (1945), *The Bachelor and the Bobby-Soxer* (1947) with Cary Grant, *That Hagen Girl* (1947) with Ronald Reagan, *Fort Apache* (1948) with John Wayne and the first screen version of *The Story of Seabiscuit* (1949), among other films. Shirley had developed into a capable actress, and critics were eager to point out that Shirley's career had successfully survived her brief retirement and the dreaded Awkward Age. "Teen Shirley" was one of the most popular actresses in Hollywood, with a huge and supportive fan base once again.

**15-year-old Shirley, star of David O. Selznick's *Since You Went Away*, in the uniform of the Westlake School for Girls.**

After marriage to actor John Agar at age 17 (their wedding was one of the most publicized events of 1945), the birth of her first child (Linda Susan) at 19 and subsequent divorce at 21, Shirley met her life mate Charles Black in 1950. They married, had two children (Charles Jr. and Lori) and remained together until his passing in August 2005. Shirley returned to the acting field in 1958 with the television series *Shirley Temple's Storybook.* The show rated excellent reviews for its contemporary retellings of classic children's stories with appearances by actors such as Charlton Heston, Arthur Treacher, Claire Bloom and Shirley herself. She entered the political arena in 1967 with a run for Congress in California, losing her bid but raising awareness of her desire to be recognized beyond the image of the world's most famous child star (whom she viewed from a healthy perspective as a beloved relative, and called "little Shirley"). Shirley Temple Black subsequently became a delegate to the United Nations General Assembly in 1969, United States Ambassador to Ghana in 1974, to Czechoslovakia in 1989 and was appointed Chief of Protocol by President Gerald Ford in 1976. She is a member of the Sierra Club and a founder of the National Multiple Sclerosis Society, after her brother George was stricken with the illness in the 1950s. She went public with her successful battle with breast cancer in 1972, urging women not to "sit home and be afraid" of a diagnosis—the first celebrity to do so in an age when the subject wasn't discussed. She wrote a best-selling autobiography *Child Star,* in 1988, outlining the first part of her life and career. She continues to be honored with awards and citations for a lifetime of work, from "little Shirley" to Ambassador Shirley Temple Black. She constantly looks forward, not backward, at her amazing life.

**Opposite: Shirley Temple Black, husband Charles and children Charles Jr., Linda Susan and Lori enjoy one of "little Shirley's" movies at their home in Atherton, California, 1957.**

Shirley TEMPLE
in THE LITTLEST REBEL
JOHN
LES
Try "THE LITTLE PRINCESS" Sundae .. 15¢
and see... "THE LITTLE PRINCESS"
STARRING SHIRLEY TEMPLE
with Richard GREENE • Anita LOUISE
Now!
Loew's STATE • Grauman's CHINESE
NATIONAL STUDIOS, INC.
228-232 West 56th Street, N. Y.
Made in U.S.
SHIRLEY TEMPLE POOR LITTLE RICH GIRL
IN PERSON FAMOUS BROADWAY COLUMNIST ED. SULLIVAN
SHIRLEY TEMPLE'S LATEST A
WITH ALICE FAYE · GLORI
ON STAGE · ED. SULLIVAN A
Ed. SULLIVAN DAWN PATROL REVUE
The POOR LITTLE RICH GIRL
SHIRLEY TEMPLE
GOODY SHOPS
Shirley Temple

# Little Miss Marquee

The majority of the movie-going public needed little persuasion to make a trip to the local theater to see a Shirley Temple film. Since first-run film releases lasted only a few days in the 1930s, long lines were part of the evening's entertainment. A wide range of colorful displays and posters distributed by the studio as well as local signmakers and display designers made the wait more palatable. Theater owners were inspired by trade publications such as *Motion Picture Herald* to create imaginative and over-the-top Shirley Temple environments for each new release. Elaborate silkscreen posters and banners lined the lobby alongside studio-issued lithograph posters; colored photographs were tacked to glass cases on the walls; life-size "standees" or cut-out figures made it seem as if Shirley herself was appearing to advertise her latest film. Promotional items were given away and kept as souvenirs by fans; upcoming releases and theater contests were heralded by images projected onscreen with the aid of glass lantern slides. Unlike today's standardized movie artwork, local signmakers in the United States and abroad weren't required to incorporate studio-issued artwork in their designs; their imaginative creations attracted the attention of Shirley's audience—both young and old—and are a tribute to the Golden Age of Hollywood.

Coming
Shirley
TEMPLE
in
LITTLE MISS BROADWAY
with
George Murphy Jimmy Durante
Shirley Temple
LITTLE MISS MIRACLE
By J. P. McEVOY
This week in...
THE SATURDAY EVENING POST
Shirley
TEMPLE
Dimples
FRANK MORGAN HELEN WESTLEY
ROBERT KENT

Displays included such items as large die-cut portraits for use on outdoor marquees, hand-colored posters, dual promotions for movies and magazine articles and spare tire covers for mobile advertising.

Shirley
TEMPLE
in
HEIDI
with
Jean
HERSHOLT

**Giveaway items included a finger puppet from Australia and an optical illusion card from Spain.**

**Opposite: Work in progress—an original com[p] sketch for the *Now and Forever* six-sheet poster.**

NOW and FOREVER
STILLS #
1004-88
1004-15
6 SHEET

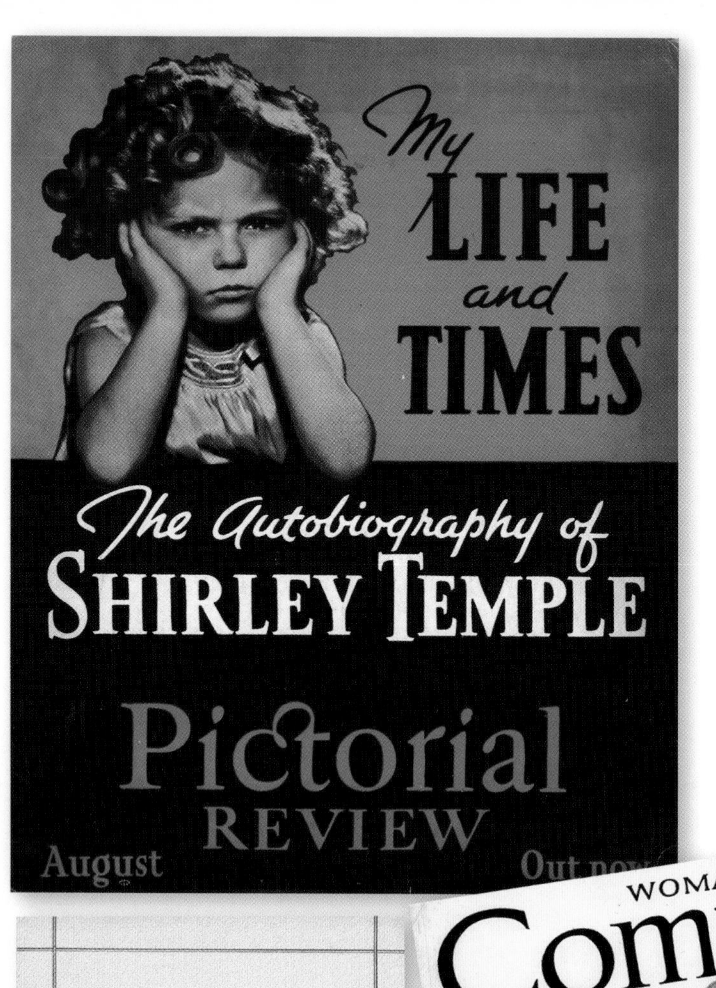
My LIFE and TIMES
The Autobiography of
SHIRLEY TEMPLE
Pictorial REVIEW
August
Out now

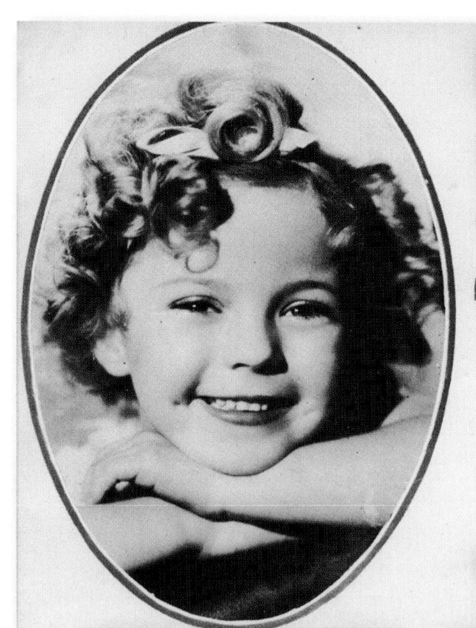
PRIVATE LIFE OF
The Wonder Ch
of The Screen--
SHIRLEY
TEMPLE
BIG FEATURE
Next SUNDAY in T
CHRONICLE

MY LIFE AND TIMES
By SHIRLEY TEMPLE
★ ★ ★
A PRE-PRINT

MY LIFE AND TIMES
Shirley-1 year
Shirley-18 mo.
Shirley-2 years
Shirley-2½ years
Shirley-4 years
Mrs. Temple-4 years
· 7 ·

WOMAN'S HOME
Companion
SHIRLEY TEMPLE
and the
BOOKS
SHE LOVES
Printed in U. S. A.

SHIRLEY Makes CHRISTMAS MERRY for CHICAGO
BALABAN & KATZ
CHICAGO THEATER
State-Randolph-Lake
Starting FRIDAY, DECEMBER 20
SHIRLEY TEMPLE
in
"The Littlest Rebel"
with
JOHN BOLES
KAREN MORLEY
BILL ROBINSON, JACK HOLT
and Gala Holiday Stage Revue
MEET ME SATURDAY
Dec. 14 . . . and Following Saturdays in the
PHOTOGRAVURE
Section of
THE CHICAGO DAILY NEWS
Every Boy and Girl, and Mother and Dad, Too, Will Want to See the Exclusive Pictures of SHIRLEY TEMPLE'S Charming Home

TODAY IS POST DAY
Is SHIRLEY TEMPLE a brat or a genius?
WHAT SORT of person is Shirley Temple, 9-year-old box-office champion of the world? Why is it almost impossible to get stars to appear in her pictures? Will she be a "has-been" at 11—or is her career just beginning? And that money she makes—how much of it will she have when she grows up? Here's the story of a million-dollar baby who has to watch her figure, who thinks a nickel is big money, and who would cost her employers $10,000 if she had a stomach ache. In the Post out today, J. P. McEvoy interviews Shirley Temple, and vice versa.
Little Miss Miracle by J. P. McEVOY

FREE
Beautiful Portrait
SHIRLEY TEMPLE
with next Sunday's
PHILADELPHIA INQUIRER
SHIRLEY TEMPLE
You do not have to go far back to find this young screen star's birth year. She was born in 1929 at Santa Monica, California. In 1933 she had already made a place for herself in Hollywood's screen firmament. Some of the pictures in which
Supplement to The Philadelphia Inqu
True Story
True Experiences
True Romances
movie mirror
Bringing up
in this month's
SHIRLEY
BY HER MOTHER
GERTRUDE TEMPLE
The American Magazine
and 30 other fascinating features
THE PICTURE STORY OF
"Shirley Temple"
Behind The Scenes With "America's Sweetheart"
A Full Photogravure Page of Pictures Each Sunday in The Des Moines Sunday Register!
Starts Sunday August 4 in
Des Moines Sunday Register


Newspapers and magazines were as eager to promote Shirley as the movie industry. Newsstand displays included die-cut and standard posters, intricate window displays, Sunday magazine inserts and pre-print articles such as the booklet on the opposite page containing *The Pictorial Review's* official 1935 Shirley Temple autobiography, *My Life and Times.*

The runaway success of *The Little Colonel* (1935) led to a renewed interest in the classic children's series by Annie Fellows Johnston. "Little Colonel" mementoes—authorized and not—abounded, including a bisque doll attired in felt from Germany (below).

LITTLE KURNELS
DELICIOUS NEW "BUILDER-UPPER" BREAKFAST CEREAL
...Ready to Eat...
WEIGHT 8 OZ. NET
The Quaker Oats Company - Chicago, U.S.A.
LITTLE COLONEL ©
HAPPY BIRTHDAY LITTLE GIRL!
STANDING AT SALUTE
IN HER HAT OF BLUE
THE LITTLE GIRL UPON THIS CARD
BRINGS
"BIRTHDAY GREETINGS"
JUST
FOR YOU!
This pop is so sweet
It reminds me of you
You are the valentine
I'd like to woo.
Added Color


Little fans could start their day with Little Kurnels, a cereal precursor to Cap'n Crunch™. Grownups could use a wooden hors-d'ouvre fork with a dangling Colonel charm at their bridge parties. Fabric, hankies and greeting cards were imprinted with artwork that looked more like Shirley than the lovely enameled brooch in blue that originated in Czechoslovakia.

The Worlds Sweetest Star
Becomes the Worlds Sweetest Doll
nly authentic Shirley Temple
the exact image of the one
y! For every little girl to
nd Forever! Here's Shirley
really is — as you love to see
her — radiant and glorious.
The world's sweetest doll! She has Shirley's
endearing smile and Shirley's laughing
and even the cute Shirley dimple. She
den curls that just match Shirley's
Her lips are Shirley's
And she's dressed in
worn by Shirley
own
(13"
SAVE TH
PICTURE F
YOUR MO
STAR ALB
THE WORLDS DARLING
TEMPLE
RLEY TEMPLE D
$2.95 to $20
$4.95
$5.95
27 inches, and every popu-
$2.95 up, our collection is complete.
over 1100 new, fresh, smiling "Shirleys"
SHIRLEY TEMPLE DOLL
PINK
Genuine
SHIRLEY TEMPLE DOLL
Clothes
Shirley Temple Dolls are Ideal Dolls

After Shirley's first feature film success in 1934, representatives from the Ideal Novelty and Toy Company of Brooklyn, New York reportedly spent several months trying to secure a contract with the Temples and design what would become one of the most popular and enduring toys of all time. The Shirley Temple doll sold in the millions during Shirley's childhood career—although the price ranged from about $2.95 for the smallest size to nearly $30 for the most elaborate version (the *Little Colonel* style shown on the opposite page).

A major part of the doll's appeal was the careful attention to detail, from the authentically-curled mohair wigs to the countless costumes adapted by designer Mollye Goldman from Shirley's own wardrobe. Mrs. Temple was very particular about the doll's appearance, especially the color of the eyes, which were custom made to match Shirley's brown shade. Legend has it that during development, Ideal's team had a special method of hitting on the perfect Shirley likeness—an employee would take a revised model home at night and carry the doll through the streets of Bay Ridge, Brooklyn. When enough neighborhood kids shouted "Hey—that's Shirley Temple!," the doll's design was approved. The final result captured the essence of Shirley—so much so, that the doll was an instant hit. Released in time for Christmas, 1934, Ideal maintained three shifts a day to keep

**Right: A test of the special rubberized primer coating on a blank body for an 11" Shirley doll. The pressed-wood composition components were dipped into the mixture to help keep the doll virtually unbreakable when new. Over time the coating would crack due to expansion and contraction of the composition base, taking the painted topcoat with it. Below right: Ideal president Morris Michtom and Shirley pose in a large portrait that hung in the factory.**

**Opposite: A skilled artisan wields a miniature curling iron to create the most recognizable doll coiffure in the world. Below: Ideal's company letterhead and a view of the Long Island City factory.**

up with the demand. Stores promoted the new doll with all the excitement of a national event. Some of the first dolls were shipped by air—a new and expensive alternative to train transport at the time. Marching bands, scores of kids and reporters anxiously awaited delivery at local airports across the country. The popularity of the Shirley Temple doll allowed Ideal, in the midst of the Depression, to move to a large building in Long Island City that became its headquarters for many years. It was topped with a spotlit billboard of Shirley facing the Long Island Railroad for the remainder of the decade—reminding all that a little child became a symbol that spurred the growth of a major company.

M. MICHTOM, President

Show Rooms
FIFTH AVENUE
NEW YORK

IDEAL NOVELTY & TOY CO.

Manufacturers of IDEAL DOLLS

CABLE ADDRESS: IDENTOY, N. Y.

SHIRLEY TEMPLE DOLLS

Main Office and Factory
23-10 43rd AVENUE, LONG ISLAND CITY, N. Y.

HOME OF "IDEAL DOLLS"

Far left: A line of workers add facial details to patiently waiting heads in one of Ideal's factory workshops. Below: An armload of curls—an unidentified Ideal employee carries a batch of identically dressed Shirley dolls to the boxing area.

THE WORLD'S DARLING
THE WORLDS DARLING
SHIRLEY TEMPLE

Three of the most popular sizes available in the 1930s, out for a stroll: 20″, 18″ and 13″. Shirley dolls were made in several sizes and price ranges, with the most affordable being a tiny 11″ size. The small doll in the green outfit was produced and distributed by Ideal's Canadian licensee, Reliable Doll and Toy. All the dolls shown here are in their original, tagged outfits with their signature Shirley Temple buttons.

THE WORLDS DARLING

Special dolls keyed to particular films were created by Ideal for display in theaters or stores. The three original dolls on the opposite page are costumed for the finale dance sequence from *Little Miss Broadway* (left), overalls and a "straw" hat for *Rebecca of Sunnybrook Farm* and a bride outfit from *Curly Top*'s "When I Grow Up" musical number. *Heidi* is shown in a Dutch outfit used in the film, mint in her original box. The hand-tinted photograph, above, shows Shirley in the same costume. It was autographed to her wardrobe mistress in 1937.

Ideal paid special attention to outfitting their army of Shirley dolls in an extensive wardrobe that was adapted from Shirley's personal and movie attire. Carefully proportioned for each size, the clothing designs were recreated in the best fabrics Ideal and designer Mollye Goldman could find. The doll's popularity soon outgrew the capacity of the factory—manufacturing Shirley doll outfits to meet demand soon became a cottage industry in the surrounding areas of Queens, Brooklyn and western Long Island. Enterprising homemakers would take in piecework using patterns and fabric supplied by Ideal; when supplies ran low, they would fan out to local merchants to find similar yardage to compensate. The workmanship was consistently excellent with nothing lost to the smallest details—hand embroidery, handkerchief edging and miles of contrasting silk ribbon. The miniature creations were then tagged with genuine Ideal Shirley Temple labels and sent back to the factory.

Authentic
SHIRLEY TEMPLE DOLL
Wardrobe Trunk
with Doll
Shirley Temple Dolls are Ideal Dolls
COPYRIGHT 1935 IDEAL NOVELTY AND TOY CO
MADE IN U.S.A.
OUR LITTLE GIRL
Ready to Travel
Popular Shirley Temple
What little girl wouldn't be delighted with this gift. So brilliant in her pretty dress, complete with trunk and extra trappings. Don't disappoint her!
4.95
Others 1.29 to 4.19
Feibleman's Fifth Floor

PLAY BEAUTY SHOP
with your
Shirley Temple Doll
Curl Her Hair in the
LATEST HOLLYWOOD STYLES
with these new doll hair wavers
Full Directions Inside
SHIRLEY TEMPLE
DOLL OUTFIT
SHIRLEY TEMPLE

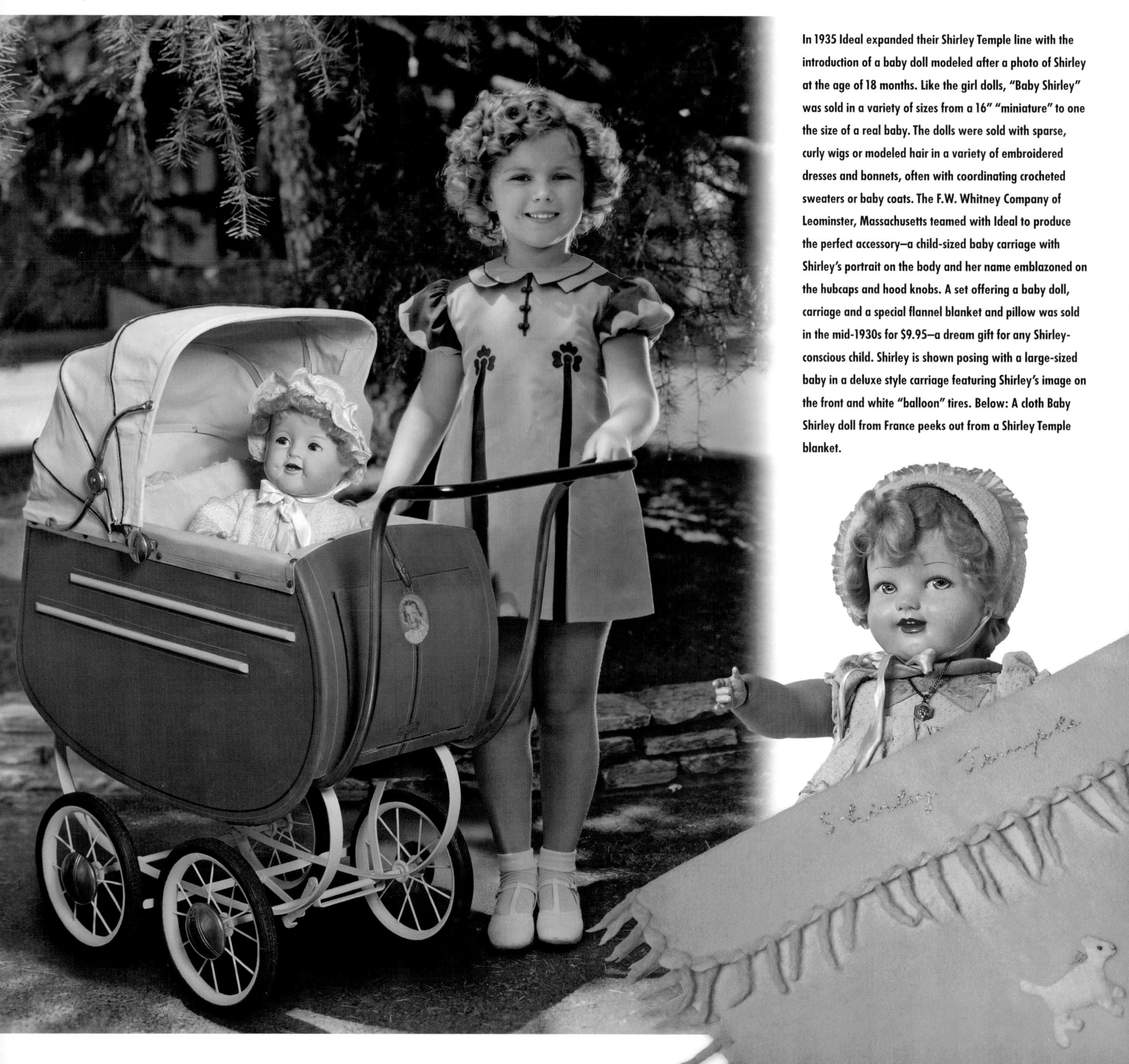


In 1935 Ideal expanded their Shirley Temple line with the introduction of a baby doll modeled after a photo of Shirley at the age of 18 months. Like the girl dolls, "Baby Shirley" was sold in a variety of sizes from a 16" "miniature" to one the size of a real baby. The dolls were sold with sparse, curly wigs or modeled hair in a variety of embroidered dresses and bonnets, often with coordinating crocheted sweaters or baby coats. The F.W. Whitney Company of Leominster, Massachusetts teamed with Ideal to produce the perfect accessory—a child-sized baby carriage with Shirley's portrait on the body and her name emblazoned on the hubcaps and hood knobs. A set offering a baby doll, carriage and a special flannel blanket and pillow was sold in the mid-1930s for $9.95—a dream gift for any Shirley-conscious child. Shirley is shown posing with a large-sized baby in a deluxe style carriage featuring Shirley's image on the front and white "balloon" tires. Below: A cloth Baby Shirley doll from France peeks out from a Shirley Temple blanket.

Shirley's doll collection grew with the addition of specially-dressed Shirley Temple dolls, sent from Fox Studio offices around the world. This example is dressed in a traditional *pollera,* the national outfit of Panama, and wears *tembleques* (spangled jewelry) in her hair.

A cloth doll from France.

"Perhaps no American toy has achieved the popularity of the Shirley Temple doll," reported *American Childhood* in 1936. "We learn that this gay little figurine is marketed in as widely separated lands as India, New Zealand, South Africa, Mexico, South America and Cuba." Ideal had wisely decided to allow manufacturers in other countries to produce and sell genuine Shirley Temple dolls in an effort to stem the scores of imitation Shirleys coming to market. An official Ideal photograph from 1936 shows licensed examples from (left to right) France, England, Poland and South America. Some of the matching dolls are shown on these two pages.

A petite doll with a celluloid head marked "Shirley Temple," made in Poland.

Australia's official Shirley dolls were sold in elaborate, lace-trimmed boxes with custom made outfits by seamstress Vera Kent.

A cloth Scottish lass from Richards, Allwin and Son of England.

A cuddly doll from Poland with a molded mask face.

An unauthorized American cloth version in a plaid coat set.

Another Allwin Art Doll example served as a pajama bag. She's shown in her original box with its label, along with her genuine British Shirley Temple doll pin.

1935
AU PRINTEMPS
UNE CRÉAT
EXCLUSIV
DU
PRINTEM
LA POUPÉE
"SHIRLEY"
dans les deux principaux costumes de la célèbre petite vedette dans le film :
LE PETIT COLONEL
à mes petits amis
de Paris
Shirley Temp
79.
99.
A PARTIR
DU JEUDI
26
NOVEMBRE
la nouvelle Shirley 1937
69F 69F 69F
AU PRINTEMPS
LA PLUS GRANDE EXPOSITION DE JOUETS DE TOUT PARIS
MODÈLE EXCLUSIF
49F
Identoy


A saucy cloth doll in a striped sweater lost her sailor hat along the way, but wears an original ID bracelet marked "Identoy" (Ideal's cable address), marking the doll as a fully authorized edition from the Au Printemps toy store, Paris.

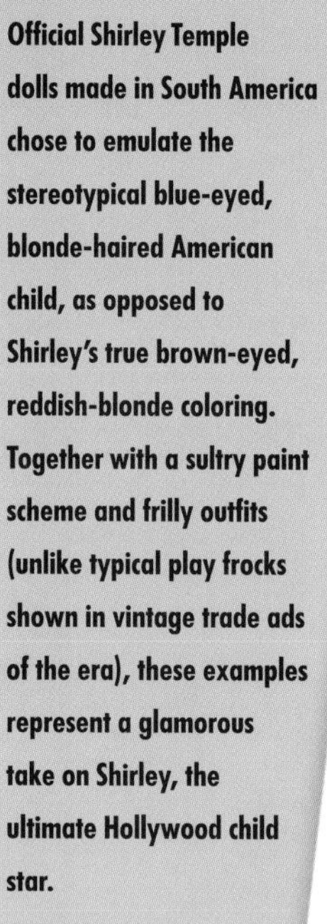

**Official Shirley Temple dolls made in South America chose to emulate the stereotypical blue-eyed, blonde-haired American child, as opposed to Shirley's true brown-eyed, reddish-blonde coloring. Together with a sultry paint scheme and frilly outfits (unlike typical play frocks shown in vintage trade ads of the era), these examples represent a glamorous take on Shirley, the ultimate Hollywood child star.**

THE WORLD'S DARLING
SHIRLEY TEMPLE
THE WORLD'S DARLING
SHIRLEY TEMPLE

Opposite: Bisque dolls from Germany and Japan face a beautifully modeled doll from the Japanese firm of Trico.

Caught between literal interpretation and caricature, celluloid Shirley dolls were produced in Germany, Japan and France. The thin, eggshell-like material was the first type of molded plastic used for production of everyday items, and perfect for showing intricate detail. The dolls were fragile playthings, however, and few survived normal use. These examples range in color from pale ivory to bright peach, all with their original clothing sewn or glued on. Production of celluloid items was phased out in the mid-1940s due to flammability of the substance.

This baby rattle with a Shirley doll face has a flapper style portrait on the reverse side.

Long and lanky boudoir dolls were more popular as bedroom décor than playthings in the 1930s. Made of cloth with molded faces, these adult-like representations of Shirley were dressed in a variety of fabrics ranging from satin to gingham. The large doll in white was produced by the French firm of Raynal, and hides a pajama bag in her ample skirt.

MOVIE BABY

Colorful figures known as "carnival dolls" show several different likenesses of Shirley. These plaster prizes won at game booths in the 1930s chipped and broke easily; today very few survive in perfect condition.

CRISP AND FRESH
POTATO
CHIPS
Joe Galler
Dealer in General Mdse.
Clothing, Furniture &
Electrical Appliances
1000 W. ROOSEVELT RD.
PHONES
Lawndale 8528
Monroe 6028-7209
1939
JANUARY
1939
SUN MON TUE WED THU FRI SAT
1 2 3 4 5 6 7
8 9 10 11 12 13 14
15 16 17 18 19 20 21
22 23 24 25 26 27 28
29 30 31
DECEMBER
FEBRUARY
HARD TO BEAT
and old
for young
A DELICIOUS TREAT

# A Household Name

From cards to china, from milk bottles to kitchen implements, from linens to potato chips to blue glass pitchers, Shirley Temple's likeness appeared in almost every home across America in the 1930s. Savvy merchandisers knew that the surest way to attract moms to their product was to attract their kids first—Shirley's recognition factor seemed to be the key to success for whatever knick-knack or gadget they wanted to sell. Shirley's parents officially licensed her name to quality manufacturers such as Hazel Atlas, (who produced the familiar blue glass giveaway items), Salem China (children's plates) and Hall Brothers (greeting cards). Despite the Temple's careful control, several renegade companies managed to make blatant use of her image, or use a lookalike that differed from Shirley only by the subtle twist of a curl. These maverick products made their way into thousands of homes via dime and department stores. The variety of items produced by these fringe manufacturers is staggering, considering that Shirley was not a cartoon character or inanimate symbol—she was a child who had attained icon status. Shirley's cheery smile was also used to sell products as varied as Quaker Puffed Wheat, Norge appliances and Dodge cars. Even Fido wasn't left out of the Shirley frenzy that swept the country—a rubber squeak toy for the family pet (shown here with a formal, personal portrait of Shirley's own Pekinese, Ching-Ching) was garbed in curls and a coat exactly like Shirley's own!

EARLY FLOWERING SPENCER
25¢
SHIRLEY TEMPLE
SWEET PEAS
MANDEVILLE Triple-Tested FLOWER SEEDS
MANDEVILLE & KING CO. • FLOWER SEED SPECIALISTS
Shirley Temple
SWEET PEA
"I'm awfully fond of sweet peas and these are beauties, with great long stems and big, pink, sweet-smelling flowers."
Aunt Jenny


A wooden garden figure poses in a field of Shirley Temple sweet peas, a variety developed and named for the star in 1935. The guardian of the garden is shown with an original snapshot taken in the yard she called home in the 1930s. The sweet peas were widely available through catalogs in seed format—as was the Shirley Temple gladiolus (pictured below with the star at an exhibit in Grants Pass, Oregon, 1936).

This 1936 Munsingwear bowl was hand-turned and decorated with Shirley in a grape arbor motif.

A lovely milk glass shell plate with a color decal bears no maker's mark.

A variety of decorative items including a cut crystal bowl, an Art Deco chrome frame and an alphabet plate marked "Bavaria."

AMERICA'S DARLING
SHIRLEY TEMPLE

SHIRLEY TEMPLE

Plasterware decor including a key holder for the kitchen and four wall plaques for a child's room (opposite).

**Pairing Shirley with pets was a popular theme: a Vogart pillow top (opposite) and an embroidered apron from Australia were sold unfinished, awaiting one's creative interpretation. The Easter card at top right was inspired by a publicity photo of Shirley with a bunny. The rubber dog toy (above) shows Shirley with a Scotty.**

The NATIONAL
PROGRAM &
PRINTING CO.
729 South Wabash Avenue
CHICAGO, ILLINOIS
Phones: Wabash 6722 - 6723

1934
PARAMOUNT THEATRE
1935
MIDDLETOWN N. Y.
Home of Paramount Pictures
Tune In on the Paramount Program, WGNY Every Saturday at 12:15 P. M.
A BROADWAY STORE ON A MIDDLETOWN STREET
William H. Tremper
CLOTHIER and FURNISHER
25 NORTH STREET
Middletown, N. Y. Dial 6919
FOR PROMPT DELIVERIES
PHONE 6600
CENTRAL COAL CO.
CITY COAL CO.
FRESH MINED COAL
20 Railroad Avenue
Scientific Eye Examination and Correct Facial Analysis
L. Mortimer Hulse
OPTOMETRIST
Where it Cost No More To Get the Best
FRANKLIN SQUARE
AHEAD
SMITH'S SHOE SHOP
Ladies' Fine Shoes a Specialty
54 North Street
Dial 7892
PACKHISER'S
CLEANERS & DYERS
EST. 1909
247-51 NORTH ST. MIDDLETOWN
Phone 7320
GRUNOW SUPER SAFE REFRIGERATORS
and GRUNOW-All Wave ....RADIOS....
Located at
113 North St. Dial 6689
Loy. C. Carter
To enjoy the Comforts of Home—Consult
William Bahntge
OIL BURNERS & OIL
BLUE FLAME RANGE OIL CO.
42 East Main St. Phone 7390
1934 DECEMBER 1934
SUN MON TUE WED THU FRI SAT
1
2 3 4 5 6 7 8
9 10 11 12 13 14 15
16 17 18 19 20 21 22
23/30 24/31 25 26 27 28 29
MIDDLETOWN WINE & LIQUOR CO.
Patronize This Store For Quality - Service and Moderate Prices
7 E. MAIN STREET
Prompt Delivery Tel. 5010
MIDDLETOWN LAUNDRY SERVICE INC.
LAUNDERERS
Phone 3404
PARTICULAR? THEN
Milady's Beauty Shop
Direction of Nellie Larkin
All Branches of BEAUTY CULTURE
42 NORTH STREET
Middletown, N. Y.
Phone 5828
Leave your prescriptions when you go to the show. We will have them ready when you return.
PARAMOUNT DRUG STORE
L. GOLDSTEIN, Prop.
Strictly a Drug Store
Open 7 Days a week till midnight
Paramount Theatre Building
Middletown, N. Y.
Get Your
INSURANCE
FROM
Lindon D. Bull
SPECIALIST
90 NORTH STREET
Middletown, N. Y. DIAL 6402

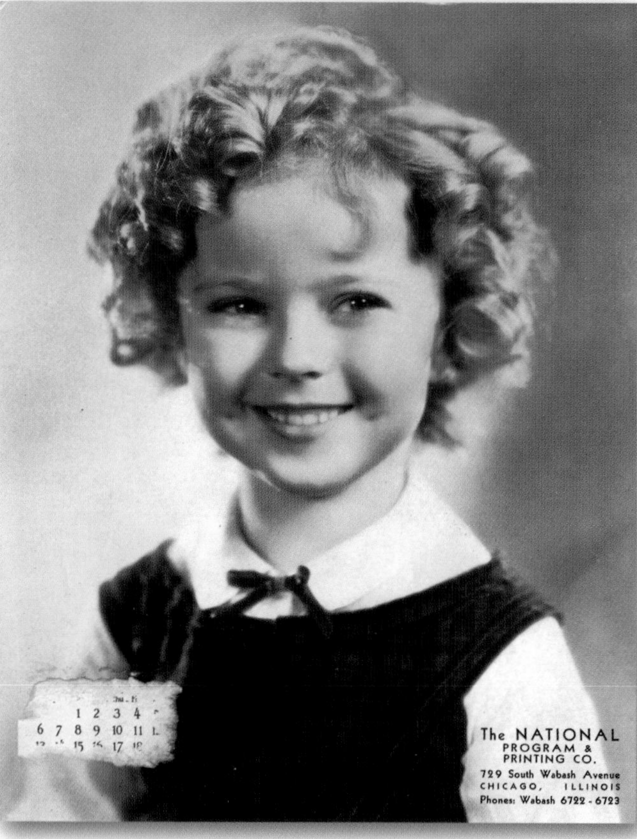

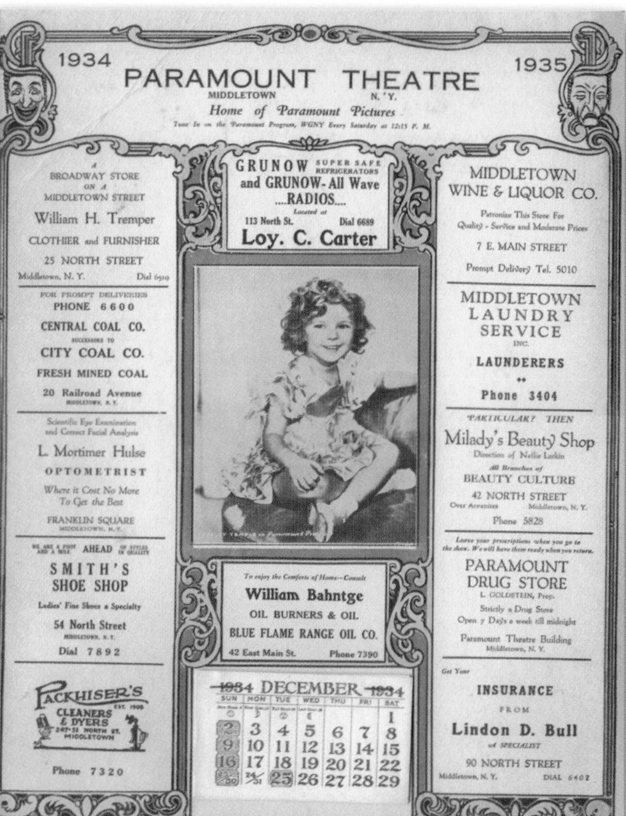

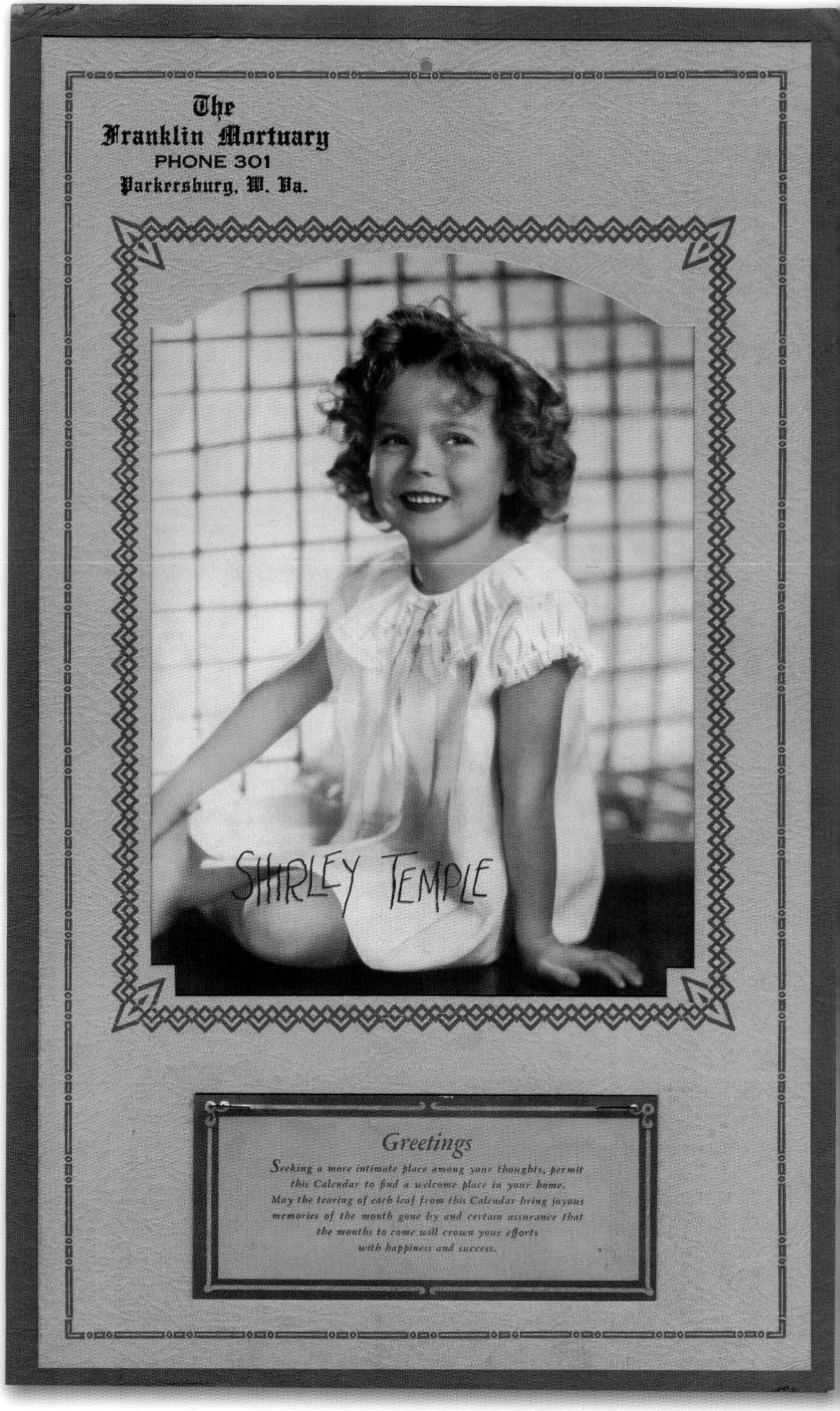

The
Franklin Mortuary
PHONE 301
Parkersburg, W. Va.
SHIRLEY TEMPLE
Greetings
Seeking a more intimate place among your thoughts, permit this Calendar to find a welcome place in your home.
May the tearing of each leaf from this Calendar bring joyous memories of the month gone by and certain assurance that the months to come will crown your efforts with happiness and success.

My Favorite
Movie Star
1938 SEPTEMB'R 1938
SUN. MON. TUE. WED. THU. FRI. SAT.
1 2 3
4 5 6 7 8 9 10
11 12 13 14 15 16 17
18 19 20 21 22 23 24
25 26 27 28 29 30


A gallery of calendars from various merchants, including the Franklin Mortuary of Parkersburg, West Virginia. The hand-colored image at right is part of a salesman's sample case for a rural photographer (below).

A mahogany plaque faces a fine china lamp by Goldsheider of Austria, a china wall plaque imitating *The Little Colonel* from Portugal and a "salt bisque" pincushion. The little figure of Shirley in her familiar curtsying pose is also found as a free-standing figure.

A bank, a mirror and a three-dimensional plaster relief picture.

In 1938, Shirley was presented with the first Automatic Electric Monophone Model #40 by the Automatic Electric Company of Northlake, Illinois. Collectors refer to this Bakelite model as the "Shirley Temple Phone." Another telephone-related item is this 1934 pocket address book with Shirley's photo on the cover.

HANDY PHONE INDEX
PATRONIZE
Loew's Triboro
AND THESE
ADVERTISERS

Paper dolls and giveaway photographs were decorated with fabric and framed during the 1930s, creating attractive wall hangings.

SCREEN GUIDE
FULL COLOR PORTRAIT of NELSON EDDY
Silver Screen
YOUNG DANCER
TIME
The Weekly Newsmagazine
MRS. TEMPLE & DAUGHTER

APRIL 1935
THE Rexall MAGAZINE
SHIRLEY TEMPLE? A PRIZE WINNER.... EASTER OR ANYTIME! YOU MAY BE, TOO, IF YOU ENTER THE MONTHLY REXALL GRAPHOLOGY CONTEST. READ ABOUT IT ON PAGE 7

The MOTORCYCLIST
OFFICIAL A.M.A. PUBLICATION
DECEMBER • Nineteen Thirty-five

Movie and RADIO GUI

Movie Go

MODERN WOMAN
A MAGAZINE PUBLISHED BY YOUR ICE COMPANY
The METROPOLITAN Host
The Timely Guide to New York

Hollywood
SPECIAL HOLIDAY NUMBER

Merry Christmas

THIS WEE IN CHICAGO

SCREENLAND
A Date with Nelson Eddy
New Shirley Temple Contest

Screen Romances

THE FAMILY CIRCLE

HOLLYWOOD EDITION
ABOUT FACES
"The NEW National Pastime"
A FASCINATING PHOTOGRAPH and CARTOON PUZZLE SERIES TESTING YOUR KNOWLEDGE OF SCREEN CELEBRITIES with an INDIVIDUAL SCORING SYSTEM

SHIRLEY TEMPLE, Chicago Theatre
Issue of June 17, 1934
Theatres
Restaurants
Where to Go
Seeing the Sights
Night Clubs
Chi Chatter
World's Fair Information

Closeups
December 1938

OVER 144 PAGES IN THIS ISSUE!
Modern Screen
"I WANT TO PLAY WITH THE QUINTS," says SHIRLEY TEMPLE

Hollywood
BRINGING UP SHIRLEY TEMPLE
PHOTOPLAY
Could You Love, Honor and Obey These Men? See Page 30

Rockefeller Center Weekly

Romantic Movie Stories

Entertainment
A MAGAZINE FOR THE FAMILY

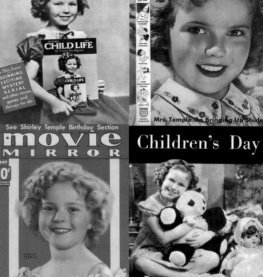

SHIRLEY TEMPLE, famous Fox Film star, depositing her pay check with her father, Geo. F. Temple, Manager of California Bank's office at Washington Street and Vermont Ave.

Patrons of the California Bank encountered this special promotional poster showing Mr. Temple proudly depositing Shirley's first Fox paycheck at the branch that he managed in Santa Monica, 1934.

Opposite: Shirley once bet a disbelieving reporter a nickel that he could pick up any magazine on a nearby table and find an article or mention of her inside. He lost. The number of Depression-era magazines featuring Shirley on the cover is staggering, and range from typical fan and household titles to *The American Motorcyclist*.

Posters, point-of-purchase displays and a wealth of comic-style ads were part of Shirley's colorful Quaker Puffed Wheat campaign. A printer's block and billboard illustration are shown above.

The successful series ran for two years in the U.S., Canada and England (where Shirley was shown enjoying Quaker Rice as well).

The Hazel Atlas Company produced the familiar blue glass pitcher, mug and bowl that almost every child of the 1930s remembers using. The three pieces were given away separately with a purchase of Bisquick or Wheaties. Opposite: A rare test style by the Hazel Atlas company used a white milk glass plate with a cobalt blue portrait of Shirley.

WHILE THEY LAST
FREE!
Shirley Temple
CHILD'S MUG
WITH ONE 40 OZ. PACKAGE OF BISQUICK at ¢
SETTING UP
A-563
THIS SIDE UP
GLASS
This was in "Curly Top" and it was supposed to be Christmas morning
Shirley Temple
Number 7 in a series of twelve Shirley Temple photos. Presented, with the cooperation of 20th Century-Fox Films, by WHEATIES, "Breakfast of Champions" with plenty of milk or cream, sugar and some kind of fruit.


The prize was outside: Wheaties was just gaining its "Breakfast of Champions" fame when the cereal company offered a series of 12 Shirley Temple cards, each printed on the back of the box.

THE BIGELOW WEAVERS

Hollywood Room Recipes

A Colonial Bedroom
adapted from
"DIMPLES"
(Twentieth Century-Fox)

SYNOPSIS OF THE PICTURE — Shirley Temple is the ragamuffin granddaughter of an old trouper, Frank Morgan, who has seen better days. They live in poor quarters on the Bowery. The scenes of the picture are laid in the middle of the 19th Century. Mr.Morgan has trained his granddaughter and a group of street urchins to dance and sing in front of saloons. Then he would offer money and help collect money from near-by men, and eventually pick the best pocket. Finally, Shirley attracts a wealthy woman, played by Helen Westley, and her fortunes change. We see her playing Little Eva in the first production of "Uncle Tom's Cabin" in New York.

DECORATIVE DETAILS — We have selected the bedroom in the stage set of "Uncle Tom's Cabin." This room is set typically in the period. We see some of the good old Colonial touches mixed with some Victorian pieces of furniture. A lovely hooked rug is on the floor. The canopied tester top Colonial bed is curtained in a wide mesh net, which would be fine if plain walls had been used. But a striped, stenciled paper was used on the walls. This paper in itself would have been excellent if a plain muslin had been used on the bed. The thing which was wrong about the room was the combining of two excellent materials which did not harmonize. The rest of the room has a couple of tables, two or three carved Victorian chairs (these are the most usable furniture heritage we have from this period), and a chest of drawers.

ADAPTING THIS ROOM — We can, of course, use the hooked rug which is just as good today as it was in those days, and we have in the Bigelow line several which are so nearly like the one in the picture, they could really be the same rug. We have selected a Beauvais rug in shades of henna-rose and blue. This rug comes in seven rug sizes up to 9x12 and in broadloom carpet up to 12 feet wide. It is colorful yet soft enough to be restful in a bedroom. It has dignity and harm enough to go with the more formal of the Federal American furnishings. We uld paint the walls and woodwork a soft medium-light shade of blue. Then we ld curtain the bed in a wide mesh net. There are many lovely new designs in lace nets of today which will make a canopied bed very attractive. The bed ld have an egg shell colored candlewick bedspread, with a simple design in the ings. The draperies would be egg shell criss-crossed organdy curtains with the es edged in blue grosgrain ribbon. The ribbon would also be used as tie backs. ssing table could be placed between the two windows or in front of a double skirted in a chintz which has henna-rose, brown, blue and white. This would simple, colorful, yet restful bedroom.

OL >>> SPRINGS BACK UNDERFOOT >>>



Relaxing at home meant that one could sit in a living room covered with a Bigelow carpet (who promoted the set designs of Shirley's films with special press kits), read the local newspaper (it almost always had a Shirley feature or photo spread) and listen to a state-of-the-art Grunow Teledial radio (it was so easy to operate that even the world's littlest star could demonstrate it!).

© COPYRIGHT 1936
Shirley Temple
lovely little 20th Century-Fox Star,
shows how easy it is to TELEDIAL!

HOLD HERE

Grunow TELEDIAL

DIAL FOR YOUR FAVORITE PROGRAM

TURN HERE

NEW Grunow "TELEDIAL TWELVE"

Only $99.95

A 12-Tube Set . . . Metal Tubes . . . 12-Inch Speaker . . . All-Wave, All-World Reception . . . Patented "Violin-Shaped" Cabinet

AND NEW Grunow "ELEVEN"

Only $69.95

An Eleven-Tube Radio at the price of a "Six"! All-Wave, All-World! Metal Tubes! Electric Eye . . . 12-Inch Speaker . . . "Violin-Shaped" Cabinet

COMMONWEALTH EDISON

**ELECTRIC SHOPS**

Downtown—72 W. Adams St. — 132 S. Dearborn St.

Telephone RANdolph 1200, Local 979

Shirley was not only the spokeschild for National Milk Week in 1937, but her image was used on milk bottles throughout the country—usually a lookalike such as the Spokane Queen of Blue Bell Dairy, shown here. Shirley also promoted Drifted Snow Flour, through a regional West Coast campaign that distributed copies of her six favorite desserts.

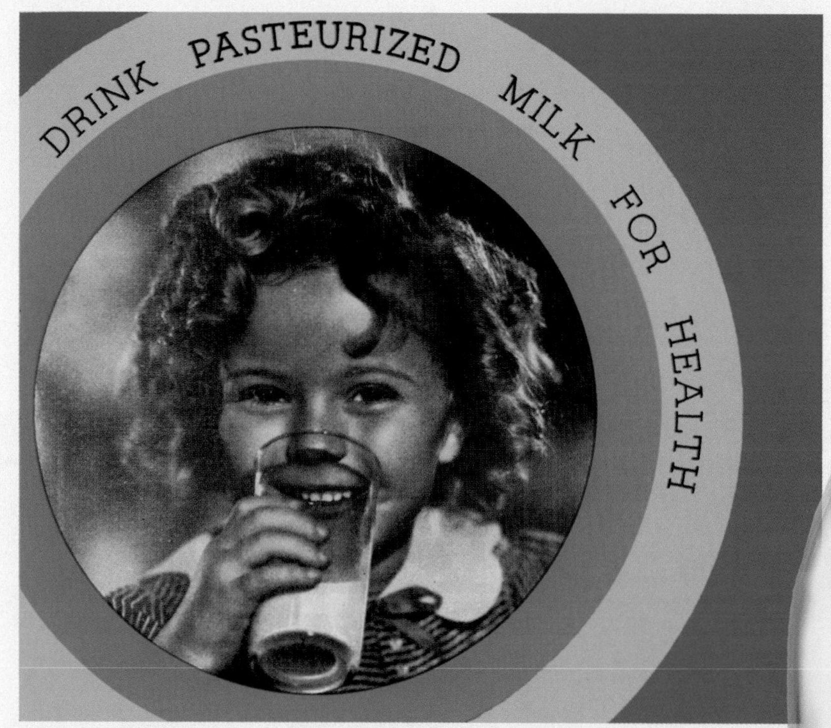

DRINK PASTEURIZED MILK FOR HEALTH
"MILK does more for the body than any other food, and does it more cheaply. It safeguards the low-cost diet for children and adults. It is the best all-around body building food."—Use it whole.
Be sure it is pasteurized.

FREE RECIPES
FOR Shirley Temple's
SIX FAVORITE DESSERTS

Martha Meade's
36
SIX-OF-A-KIND
RECIPES

36 MORE RECIPES!
These six Shirley Temple desserts are just a sample of the novel "Six-of-A-Kind" foods you'll find in Martha Meade's book of 36 recipes ... given free inside every sack of Drifted Snow Flour

DRIFTED SNOW
FLOUR
"Home Perfected"

TAKE ONE

Shirley Temple's SIX FAVORITE DESSERTS
To make these desserts exactly as Shirley prefers them, be sure to use Drifted Snow, the "Home-Perfected" flour!

CURLY TOP'S FAVORITE

Apple Custard

Peanut Butter Crumb

SHIRLEY'S SEVENTH BIRTHDAY CAKE

Orange Custard

Coconut Frosting

HOLLYWOOD SHORTCAKE

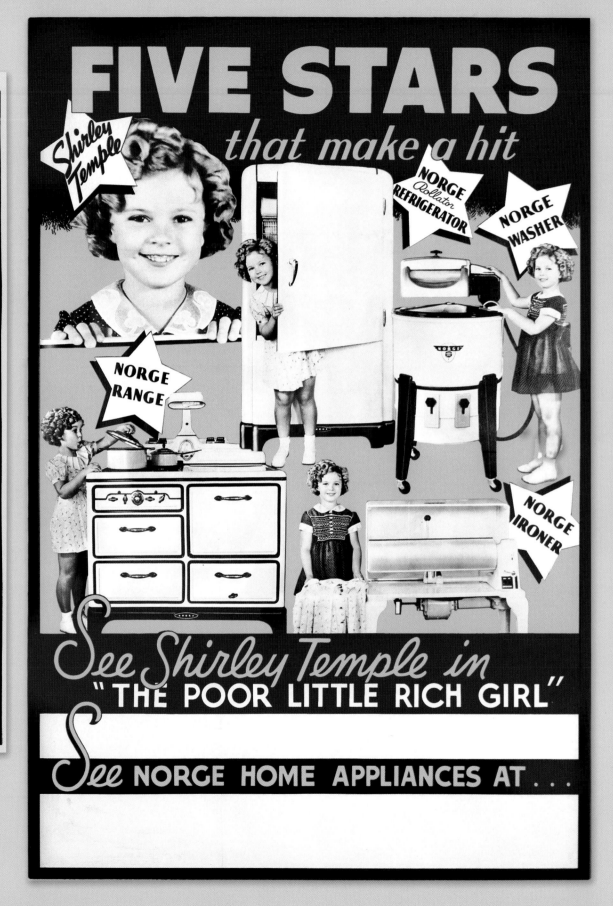


A San Jose, California appliance store used Shirley's signature phrase to sell Westinghouse refrigerators in 1934; a couple of years later Shirley promoted Norge appliances in conjunction with her film *The Poor Little Rich Girl*.

FIVE STARS
that make a hit
Shirley Temple
NORGE Rollator REFRIGERATOR
NORGE WASHER
NORGE RANGE
NORGE IRONER
See Shirley Temple in
"THE POOR LITTLE RICH GIRL"
See NORGE HOME APPLIANCES AT . . .

"A safe car for Shirley Temple" was this Dodge model, supposedly chosen by Mrs. Temple to transport her daughter back and forth to the studio. Shirley was presented with the first production model for 1936; she happily posed with the auto on the *Littlest Rebel* set. Reprints of the photo were sent out to consumer requests.

DODGE

Your little girl and
"OUR LITTLE GIRL"
"Our Little Girl," starring Shirley Temple, has started a vogue in filmland—in fashionland, too!
Authentic Shirley Temple Undies
131 W. 35th St. New York
$1.50
Per Pair
"you'll love this sweater, too" Shirley Temple
An Exclusive KnitTown Creation
EACH COAT BEARS A SHIRLEY TEMPLE LABEL
"THE GLOVE I LOVE" Shirley Temple 20TH CENTURY-FOX FILM STAR
Shirley Temple
reproduction of this style worn by SHIRLEY TEMPLE
a CINDERELLA frock

Shirley Temple set the fashion pace for little girls in the midst of the Depression years. Despite the universal perception of a curly-headed little girl with a closet full of fussy party dresses, Shirley's personal wardrobe was smartly styled and tailored, from formal silk frocks to everyday cotton play suits or overalls. Styled by studio designers such as Gwen Wakeling and René Hubert, Shirley's garments showed imaginative attention to detail and color. Her outfits were adapted for sale under the Shirley Temple Brand banner—a co-op of companies that produced socks, shoes, underwear, hats, purses, swimsuits, coats, raingear, jewelry, bathrobes, scarves, gloves and hairbows—all of the highest quality and sold under license from the Temples and Fox. A huge array of advertising material was utilized to attract the young fashion set, resulting in fabulous window displays often featuring elaborate mannequins that resembled Shirley herself. Meanwhile, the object of this fashion swirl was dutifully trying on each frock or hat for Mrs. Temple's approval, and for the hangtags that declared the garment to be "Just Like Mine."

The Shirley Temple Cinderella Frock line was the most successful of all the Shirley Temple Brand fashions. In a fortunate

**Sidney Rosenau would often visit Shirley in California, sometimes becoming the subject of a fashion shoot himself.**

move, the Rosenau Brothers of Philadelphia had chosen Shirley to model a line of "Hollywood 2-in-1" playsuits during her Educational career; when her star began to rise it was natural that one of the company's founders, Sidney Rosenau, would seek a long-term license from the Temples. The dresses were of the highest quality—even when offered by catalogs such as Sears, the prices were twice those of a regular child's frock. The line was also successfully exported to the United Kingdom, where a little Shirley wannabe modeled the fashions for the press. The Temple-Rosenau association lasted long after Shirley's childhood film career—company files showed concepts for a line of dresses to be sold during her teenage years; unfortunately, they were never produced. When Shirley re-emerged on television in the late 1950s, the company again produced a line of contemporary clothing under the Shirley Temple name, including a series of mother-daughter fashions.

**Opposite: Various mementoes from the Cinderella Frock line, including brochures, a doll-sized promotional frock emblazoned with the Cinderella coach logo, a company-issued paperweight and a brass figure in a snappy frock that possibly sat on a desk in one of the Rosenau factories of Central Pennsylvania.**

LEY TEMPLE
mous child star of ★
ATIONAL PICTURES'
CS OF YOUTH COMEDIES
wearing her
OLLYWOOD 2-IN-1"
SUN-SHORT
"HOLLYWOOD
2-IN-1'S"
PANTY DRESS
SUN-SHORT
(to match)
Cinderella Frocks
"HOLLYWOOD 2-IN-1's"
• a pantie dress •
• a matching sun-short •
Cinderella Frocks
Set the Fashion for Smart Back-to-School Wear
a cinderella frock
SHIRLEY TEMPLE
BRAND
CINDERELLA'S COACH
Into the New Year
with a new triumph!
1937
SHIRLEY TEMPLE
TWENTIETH CENTURY-FOX FILM STAR

Various dress tags produced throughout Shirley's childhood.

A large window display poster showing a popular style from ***The Little Colonel***.

Overleaf: a very small fraction of the Shirley Temple Cinderella Frocks produced during the 1930s.

Wonder Tot
SHIRLEY TEMPLE

*Wonder Tot*

Imaginative store windows included a lineup of live models, all wearing Shirley Temple frocks; most clutch simple dolls while the older girls enjoy a tea party. Right: A cardboard mannequin outfitted in flowers graces this postcard from England. Below: A generic framed and colored photograph could be utilized as part of a Shirley Temple Brand display.

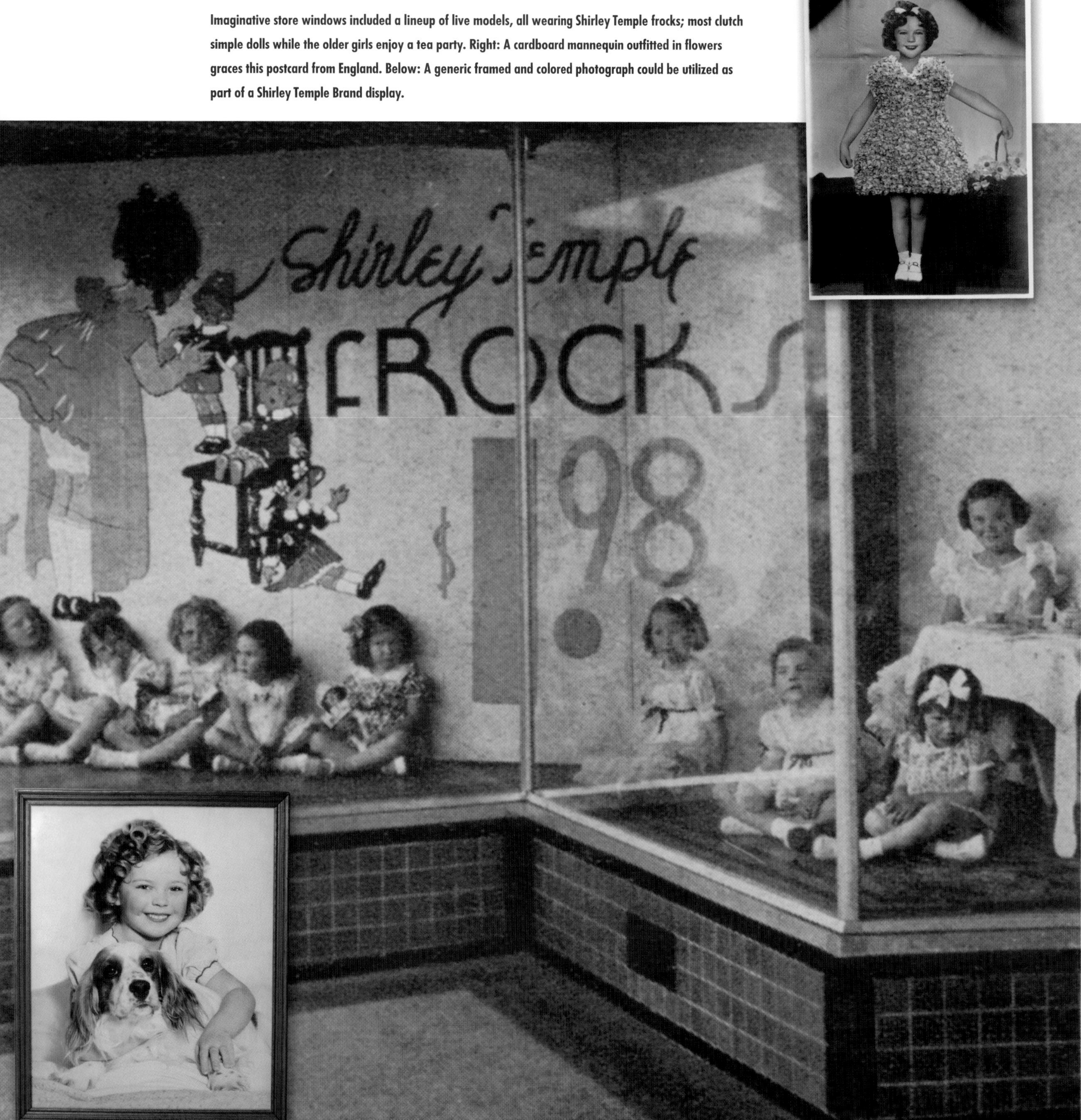

A fantasy window display features a life-sized mannequin from Italy (left) and her American counterpart. The stunning model from Milan wears a generic silk dress from Europe, while the sporty-looking U.S. version wears a genuine Shirley Temple dress. The hand-colored poster in the background would have been

a handful of Easter "honeys" worn by

Shirley Temple

in "Captain January"

Now Showing at the New Theatre

...All Here At Hochschild, Kohn & Co.

Let your little girl enjoy these adorable frocks which make Shirley Temple so completely irresistible! The tag-photograph on each garment shows how Shirley looks in the very same style.

**authentic Shirley Temple Fashions:**

Dresses .......... 1.95
Beach Outfits .......... 1.95
Raincoats .......... 3.99
Undies .......... 1.19 and 2.25
Silk Hats .......... 3.50
Socks .......... 35c. 3 prs. 1.00
Handbags .......... 1.00
Slippers .......... 1.00
Dolls .......... 2.95 to 12.95

— A Shirley Temple Gift —

NOW ON DISPLAY...
New
Shirley Temple
Dresses
—at—
$1.95
In a Most Complete Showing
in all the Lovely Sheer Pastels
Sizes 3 to 6½
SHIRLEY TEMPLE DRESSES are made by the manufacturers of Cinderella Frocks for little girls . . . this line has been carried by Ramsay's for years . . . offering you the latest and smartest creations at all times.
FREE SHIRLEY TEMPLE
PHOTO
WITH EACH DRESS
Always Ahead
in New Kiddies' Wear.
Ramsay's
The Dominant Retail Institution of Pittsburg

Cinderella's
AUTUMN LEAVES
OF STYLE
SHIRLEY TEMPLE
SCHOOL FROCKS
Never have we shown such a variety of smart Fall styles for girls..."Highland Fling" ensembles with matching "Scottie" hats, swirling skirt Spun Rayon prints new in texture and design . . . and so many other beautiful, washable* Shirley Temple styles. Hurry in while assortments are complete.
*Ivory Flakes or other mild soap suggested.
$1.98
• Left: "Highland Fling"; suspender-top skirt, separate jacket, matching "Scottie" hat. Woven plaid Spun Rayon blended with Cotton. Shirley Temple style, sizes 4-6½; 7-14.
• Right: Charming floral print Crown tested Spun Rayon. Two-tone piping, gored skirt, embroidered linen collar. A Shirley Temple style, sizes 3-6½; 7-12.
LOOK FOR CINDERELLA'S COACH
THE SIGN OF SMART FROCKS FOR GIRLS
DAMON'S
SECOND FLOOR

celebrating the arrival of adorable
new summer styles . . . SHIRLEY TEMPLE
BIRTHDAY FROCKS
$1.98
Big and Little Sister Dressed Smartly Alike . . . a new idea in young fashions adapted to this gay nautical Shirley Temple style. Navy or red trims both mess jacket and the backless sport dress underneath of white cotton shantung. Sizes 8-12.
Birds and Flowers . . . flirt all over cross-bar muslin print, with pleated collar. Sizes 3 to 6½.
Froth of Organdy . . . with full, fulf-banded skirt, rosebud, blue, pink, with matching posies. 3 to 12.
Girls' Toggery and Infants' Departments—Fifth Floor.


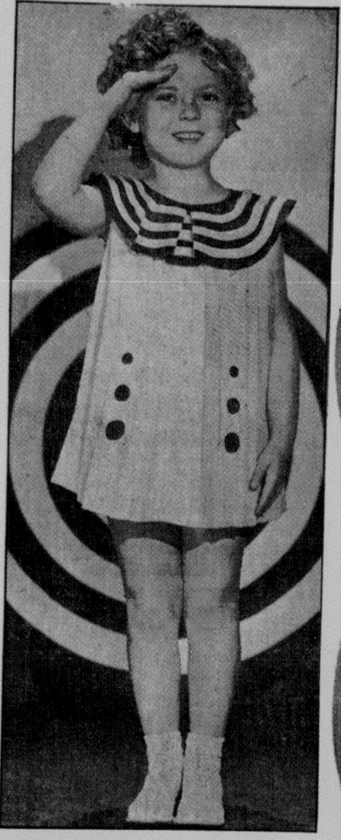

Hollywood's Darling Sets Young America's St
Here are the only
AUTHENTIC
Shirley Temple
Fox Film Star
FROCKS
made under exclusive right by
cinderella
When America's best beloved little girl wears a new frock every other youngster wants one just like it. Mothers, too, will like these Sports Togs in piques, linens and other sporty fabrics as well as the playtime styles in sheers and tissue ginghams with their dainty touches of handwork. Sizes 3 to 6, 7 to 10.
1.98
ABOVE: This style is named "Little Colonel." It's fine white pique trimmed with appliques of bright navy. 3 to 6 years .......... 1.98
This and the six other styles (not illustrated) were made expressly for Shirley Temple. See them! They're fascinating for your little girl. Sizes 3 to 6 years .......... 1.98
—Maison Blanche Second Floor

**Shirley Temple Soap Dolls**

**59c**

Cunning miniatures of the popular little movie star in soap to delight her little admirers.

*HOLMES TOILETRIES—*
*First Floor*

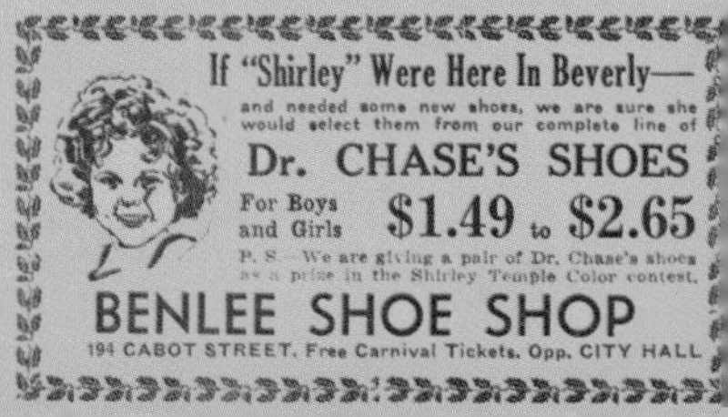

If "Shirley" Were Here In Beverly—

and needed some new shoes, we are sure she would select them from our complete line of

**Dr. CHASE'S SHOES**

For Boys and Girls **$1.49 to $2.65**

P. S.—We are giving a pair of Dr. Chase's shoes as a prize in the Shirley Temple Color contest.

**BENLEE SHOE SHOP**

194 CABOT STREET. Free Carnival Tickets. Opp. CITY HALL

Promotional items and newspaper ads surround an image of Shirley riding Cinderella's coach—"The Sign of Smart Frocks for Girls." The special edition of *Shirley Temple's Birthday Book*, below, celebrated Rosenau Brothers' 20th anniversary.

SHIRLEY TEMPLE

FALL COATS & SNOW SUITS

MADE UNDER EXCLUSIVE RIGHTS by

H&B

Every Coat & Snow Suit with a "SHIRLEY TEMPLE" Label

Lined with "EARL GLO"

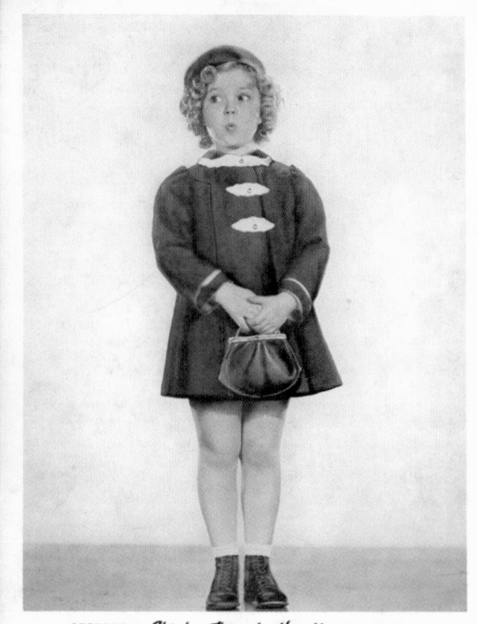

**A small selection of the huge variety of display items for Shirley Temple fashions, including coats, snowsuits, socks, swimsuits and hats. "Earl Glo," featured in the coat poster on this page, was a special synthetic lining that shimmered in the light when the garment was opened.**

Shirley Temple Hats by Lewis
BACK TO SCHOOL
WITH
Shirley Temple
TWENTIETH CENTURY—FOX STAR
Cinder
Frocks
SHIRLEY TEMPLE SNOWSUIT
EACH SNOWSUIT BEARS A SHIRLEY TEMPLE LABEL
Authentic
SHIRLEY TEMPLE
Bathing Suits
by
FOREST MILLS
authentic
SHIRLEY TEMPLE SOCKS
by Trimfit

**Miscellaneous Shirley Temple accessories to round out a fashionable girl's wardrobe, many in their original boxes with tags.**

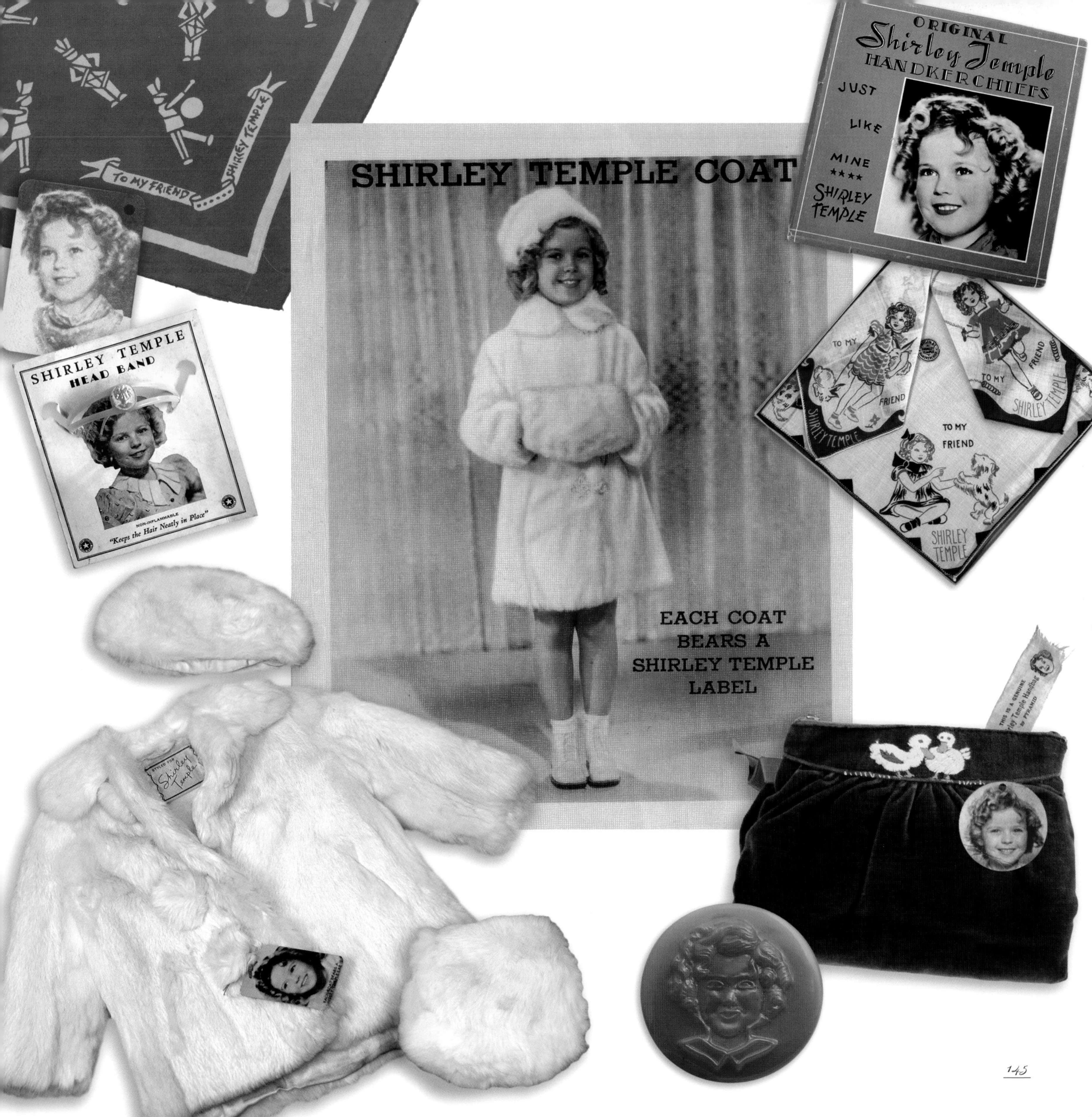
TO MY FRIEND
SHIRLEY TEMPLE
ORIGINAL
Shirley Temple
HANDKERCHIEFS
JUST
LIKE
MINE
★★★★
SHIRLEY TEMPLE
SHIRLEY TEMPLE COAT
EACH COAT
BEARS A
SHIRLEY TEMPLE
LABEL
SHIRLEY TEMPLE
HEAD BAND
NON-INFLAMMABLE
"Keeps the Hair Neatly in Place"
TO MY
FRIEND
SHIRLEY TEMPLE
TO MY
FRIEND
SHIRLEY TEMPLE
TO MY
FRIEND
SHIRLEY
TEMPLE
STYLED FOR
Shirley Temple

Shirley Temple soap novelties were created by noted display designer (and soap sculptor) Lester Gaba for Kerk Guild in the mid-1930s.

Undies, pajamas and robes were produced by Gem Baby Wear of New York City. The glamorous robe, above, survived in perfect condition because its original owner couldn't afford to have it dry cleaned on a regular basis!

The finishing touch: jewelry produced by Monocraft of Rhode Island. The large plaster maquette, opposite, was the original model used to create the small charm of Shirley and her Scotty shown above left. Beautifully packaged and presented, the line featured a series of charms or "dangles" available separately for its child-sized bracelets, each with its own poem: "Here's a lovely dangle / Shiny, bright and new / Wear one on your bracelet / Shirley wears one too."

Shirley Temple on the Movie Lot
SHIRLEY'S BUNGALOW
SAALFIELD PUB. CO. AKRON, OHIO
Shirley Temple
PAINTS and CRAYONS
SHIRLEY TEMPLE CRAYONS
Shirley Temple standing Dolls
AUTHORIZED ···EDITION···
FRONT
BACK
No. 1715
SHIRLEY TEMPLE
Favorite
PUZZLES
STUDIO
TWINKLE TWINKLE LITTLE STARS OF HOLLYWOOD
ENTER
Shirley Temple
There are temples and temples
Over the sea,
But we have a Temple—
Lovely is she!
CAN YOU FIND THE WAY TO SHIRLEY'S BUNGALOW?

# Paper Playmate

The fact that Shirley was considered a happy, smart kid (a Stanford University Binet test rated Shirley a "super genius" at age seven) didn't prevent some media outlets from a mild state of panic over her work versus play situation. She was branded a "wage slave" by the *Sunday Worker* newspaper, but nothing was farther from the truth. She loved to work, and loved to play—Mrs. Temple and her teacher Klammie made sure she had time for both. Shirley loved to draw and "craft" between scenes on the set and on vacation—to the point of reporters predicting an artistic career in her future. While Shirley was expressing herself creatively in the eons-away world of movie studios and Palm Springs, thousands of children around the globe were inspired by reproductions of her drawings and schoolwork in magazines and newspapers. These young fans in turn could play with authorized Shirley Temple children's activity books published by the Saalfield Company of Akron, Ohio. Their books, coloring sets, paper dolls and construction sets are among the most visually lovely series ever produced for children. The Shirley Temple line was designed by the husband and wife team of Corinne and Bill Bailey, working with specially posed and colored photographs as illustrations—Shirley was as interactive with the creation of these books as the artists. The

series was extremely successful in the mid-1930s; so much so that the company business cards used miniature front and back covers of a Shirley Temple coloring book. The Temples themselves made a special stop at the Saalfield plant on their 1938 cross country trip to greet A.G. Saalfield, president of the firm, and his wife. By that time, 40 million of the Shirley Temple books had been published. If kids couldn't go to Hollywood to play with Shirley, the Saalfield books were an excellent substitute.

Manufacturers around the world issued their own Shirley Temple rainy day playthings, some artistic and some wildly creative, most unauthorized. Comic books produced in France and Spain put Shirley on the same adventurous level as Little Orphan Annie—their Shirley characters found themselves in any number of episodes that would have made rough-and-tumble Shirley smile.

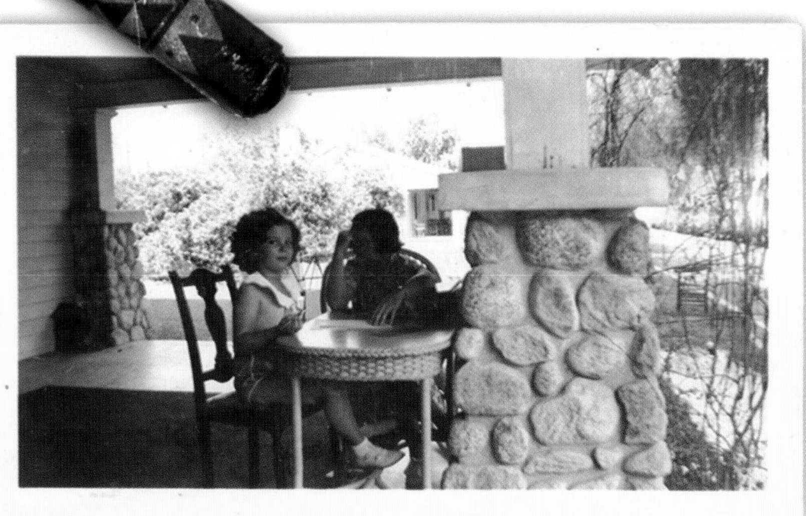

**Quiet moments (such as this lesson break on a porch in Palm Springs with Klammie) often produced carefully crayoned novelettes. "Miss Moony Cat," opposite, is an eight-page example given to Shirley's bodyguard, Grif, in 1936.**

Teacher Klammie accompanied the Temple family on their local trips to Palm Springs, giving Shirley a sense of continuity (and homework) during between-films downtime. Photographs show Shirley on a wide porch, doing her lessons or cutting and pasting paper gifts for her friends. Valentine and Christmas cards were also created by the young star with her interest in crafting her own holiday greetings leading to "how-to" articles in movie magazines.

Other items with play value included picture books featuring biographies of famous child stars (*Twinkle, Twinkle Little Stars of Hollywood*), pre-Viewmaster film strips using early film clips of Shirley in *The Red-Haired Alibi*, and scrapbooks with Shirley's picture on the cover so young crafters could start their own Shirley Temple archive.

published
by Shirley
Temple.

Miss Moony
Cat

Wonder Tot
PUBLICATIONS OF THE SAALFIELD PUBLISHING COMPANY
SHIRLEY TEMPLE BOOKS
Authorized Editions
10 Cent Retail
Of course, the entire city knows that Shirley Temple was in town. With her in this photo, reading left to right, is her mother, Mrs. George Temple, Mr. Temple, A. G. Saalfield and Mrs. Saalfield. Shirley visited the Saalfield Publishing Co. where 40,000,000 Shirley Temple books have been published.
Giving the Public What It Likes
SHIRLEY TEMPLE
A line of merchandise promising unlimited sales opportunity for both the Toy and Book Departments.
Shirley Temple Story Book
SHIRLEY TEMPLE Story Book
SHIRLEY TEMPLE PASTIME BOOK
SHIRLEY TEMPLE
SHIRLEY TEMPLE


Saalfield hardcover books, surrounded by a 1937 company catalog (above), a trade ad (below left), a clipping showing the Temple's visit to the plant and a pair of plaster bookends, crafted by a fan in the 1930s.

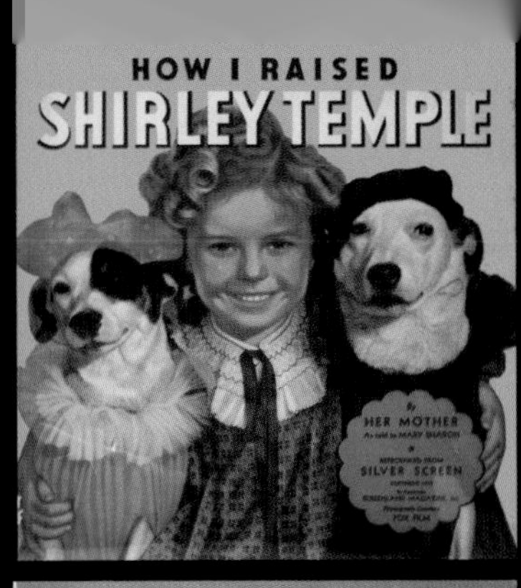

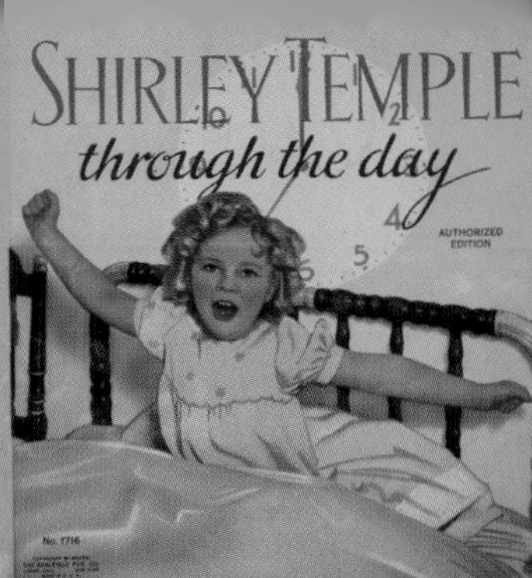

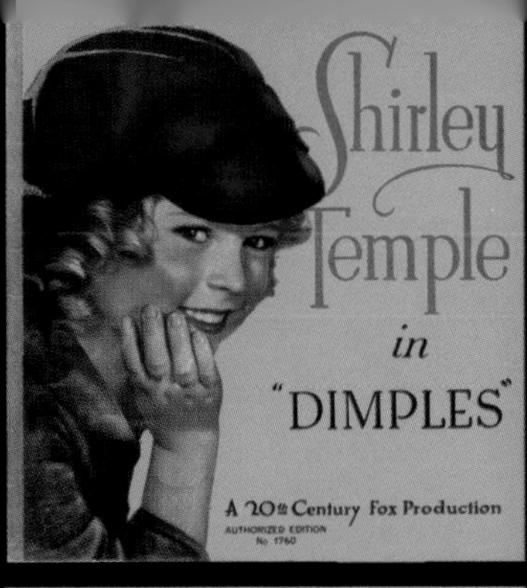

Now I am
Eight
by Shirley
Temple
AUTHORIZED
EDITION

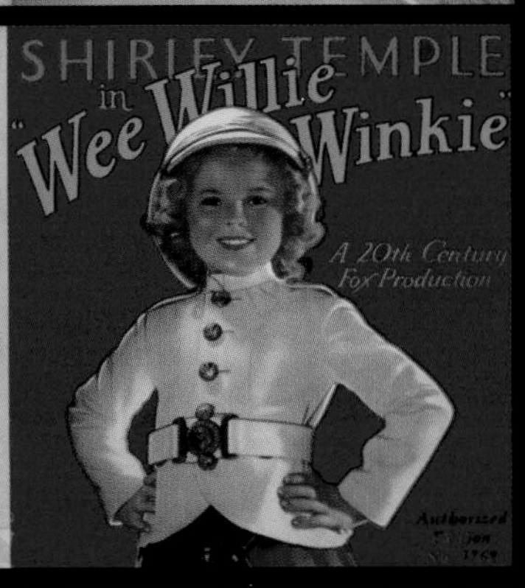

SHIRLEY TEMPLE
in "Wee Willie Winkie"
A 20th Century
Fox Production

Shirley Temple in
HEIDI
A 20th Century
Fox Production

SHIRLEY TEMPLE
in THE LITTLE PRINCESS
A 20th Century
Fox Production
AUTHORIZED EDITION

SHIRLEY TEMPLE IN
SUSANNAH of the MOUNTIES
A 20th Century
Fox Production
AUTHORIZED
EDITION

Saalfield storybooks, including editions licensed to publishers in Denmark and France. The box at right contained discontinued items.

A selection of children's activity books published by Saalfield.

SHIRLEY TEMPLE
Drawing Book
Authorized Edition
PERMANENT FILE COPY
RETURN PROMPTLY TO
LIBRARY DESK
ST
1725
SHIRLEY TEMPLE
Authorized Edition
My Coloring Box
These are my own pictures of my own things which I love
Shirley Temple.
Shirley
SHIRLEY TEMPLE
Christmas Book
No. 1770
Shirley Temple's Sewing Cards
SHIRLEY'S
BEACH PAIL
THIS IS MY CRAYON BOOK
Shirley Temple
No. 287

**A sample of Saalfield's paper doll sets, including an exact reproduction of Shirley's early backyard playhouse (below and opposite).**

Two different, doll-sized china tea sets from pre-war Japan feature caricatures of Shirley on each lustreware component.

A 1939 how-to article for kids showing the same type of valentines taken from Grif and Mabel's scrapbook.

Opposite: A hand-cut and crayoned valentine from Shirley to the Griffiths, including a handwritten envelope.

TO MY
HAVE I A LOOK-IN?
I WANT TO BE YOUR VALENTINE!
TO MY VALENTINE
To Grif and Mabel
Love,
Shirley Temple
WOODEN-SHOE LIKE TO BE MINE VALENTINE?

FOR children only

I'VE ALWAYS PICTURED YOU-

AS MY VALENTINE— HOW ABOUT IT?

This is the outside of one of the "cut-out" valentines made by Shirley Temple

Inside of same valentine. Letters are painted in water color, bears pasted on

By GORDON BARRINGTON

FOR several years now Shirley Temple has made her own valentines. At present she is busily engaged with paper, scissors, paste and crayons, fashioning this year's valentines, which, she tells us, will number nearly 75.

At the top of Shirley's valentine list are, of course, her "Mummie" and her "Daddy." After them, in order, come her two brothers, her little playmates, and then her many motion picture friends in Hollywood.

If the little 20th Century-Fox star is performing in a picture at the Valentine season, she remembers the people who have worked with her. Recently her studio completed the filming of *The Little Princess*, with Shirley as the star. I found when I visited her that she is working in-

Here is Shirley at work on valentines for this year. Last year's valentine to her father is shown at lower left

Shirley ... asked her if she would ... hints on "how to mak...

"I just make each one ... to me," she responded ... how the ideas come. I ... children make their ow... and I'm su... ideas ab...

... good ... think of anything ... Goodness knows, lots of people wo... what my pictures are supposed to be! But ... everyone would rather ... something, no mat-... make are all very ... ladies' valentines I ... bouquet of flowers, ...

[Continued on page 85]

...s to fold as shown. Then ... pass ribbon through and tie

WHITE PAPER

COLORED PAPER

Write or draw picture inside folding hearts. Edges may ... decorated with lace, tin f...

After sentiment has been written within hearts, fold together make holes on left hand side and pass ribbon through

# MAKING VALENTINES WITH SHIRLEY TEMPLE

36

To
Mr. and Mrs
Griffith

To My Valentine
To Mr. and mrs.
Griffith.
love
Shirley Temple.

Cut paper Christmas trees folded to stand up; these were created by Shirley as well as the construction paper tulip at right.

A woodcraft miniature magazine rack appears to have been signed by Shirley (see top image) and dated 1939; it's possible this was a craft done during her Campfire Girl days.

Free time also involved autographing a limited amount of photos for fans; secretaries took care of some of the requests. This was signed by Shirley in 1934.

Opposite: A vintage oilcloth hassock for a child's room.

**Comic books from Spain (above) and France featured Shirley characters that were allowed more derring-do than their real-life inspiration. The Spanish books paired Shirley with Toni, a little boy. The 1942 annual at right shows Shirley and her fellow icon, Mickey Mouse. The 1938 French comic, above, was one of a series of four.**

Kids in 1930s England could drive their mothers mad by putting these Shirley Temple decals everywhere!

April 10th

I'm going to have a birthday party April 25 and want you to come to it.

love
Shirley Temple

SHIRLEY TEMPLE'S
8th Birthday Party
20th-Century Fox Studio
April 1937

# Monday's Child

Birthdays are a social rite of passage for any kid. If you were a star with the status of Shirley Temple, however, that event took on the scope of a national holiday. Besides marking the year gone by and the prospect of growing up, the unique celebration of Shirley Temple's birthday during her childhood emphasized the accomplishments of such a young child—especially with her studio-imposed age at a year younger than she actually was (changing her from a Monday child to a Tuesday baby). From a marketing standpoint, the proximity of April 23rd to the Easter holidays lent itself to special promotions of Shirley Temple-branded items and the release of her latest film. From a personal standpoint, the milestone meant that Shirley presided over a mega-bash that was usually closed to the press and held in the Fox Studio commissary (such as the one for her "eighth" birthday, pictured). Engraved invitations in Shirley's

**Elegant children from a New Jersey dancing school pose on the Atlantic City boardwalk while signing an oversized postcard to greet Shirley on her birthday in 1936.**

handwriting allowed access by 200-or-so children of the Hollywood press corps, directors and luminaries—most of whom Shirley did not know. Close friends such as her stand-in, the Chaplin boys, the Harold Lloyd children and Darryl Zanuck's girls were invited to this party and a much smaller, private one at Shirley's home. Those who attended the studio fete were wined and dined on ice cream and a magnificent cake; gifted with exclusive favors such as a mechanical pencil/magnifying glass gadget with Shirley's autograph; photographed for posterity at their tables and treated to a floor show, often featuring the tap dancing of Bill Robinson. Manufacturers also produced items in homage to Shirley's birthday, such as a Japanese-made tin whistle with a caricature of the star, so kids all over the world could have their own Shirley Temple party.

**Opposite: Shirley's 1935 "sixth" birthday party at the Fox studio was modest in comparison to those held starting the following year. The decorations and cake were fairly simple and more like those of the average child. Inset: Shirley was a favorite subject for pre-war British birthday postcards.**

Shirley Temple
EIGHT happy years! Here's many more
Still happier than you've had before.
R. 270

Shirley's birthday took on the scope of a national holiday. Department stores and theaters in towns across America outdid themselves in sending impressive greetings to the star in Hollywood, all beautifully crafted and eagerly signed by what seemed like the entire town population. Would Shirley see your name? Probably not, but at least one store in Houston sent out a "thank you" postcard, right, to all who signed Shirley's birthday book—as if the card came from Shirley herself.

Opposite: Birthday cards from the U.S. and overseas, along with a hand-painted envelope postmarked from the town of Shirley, Virginia.

**Mayor Wells' Children Are First to Sign Shirley Temple's Birthday Card**

Shirley
DAVENPORT WISHES YOU THE HAPPIEST OF BIRTHDAYS

Davenport's first son and daughter, Nancy and George Wells, children of Mayor and Mrs Merle Wells, make certain that they'll be the first to send birthday greetings to Shirley Temple, famous child film star who will celebrate her sixth birthday April 23, by signing a giant birthday card to be sent to her by the children of Davenport.

Other Davenport kiddies will have an opportunity to sign the giant card at the Shirley Temple birthday party at the Capitol theater Saturday morning at 11 o'clock. They will see one of Shirley's favorite pictures, "Baby Take a Bow," in addition to the Capitol's regular attractions. Free prizes and gifts are promised for all the children.

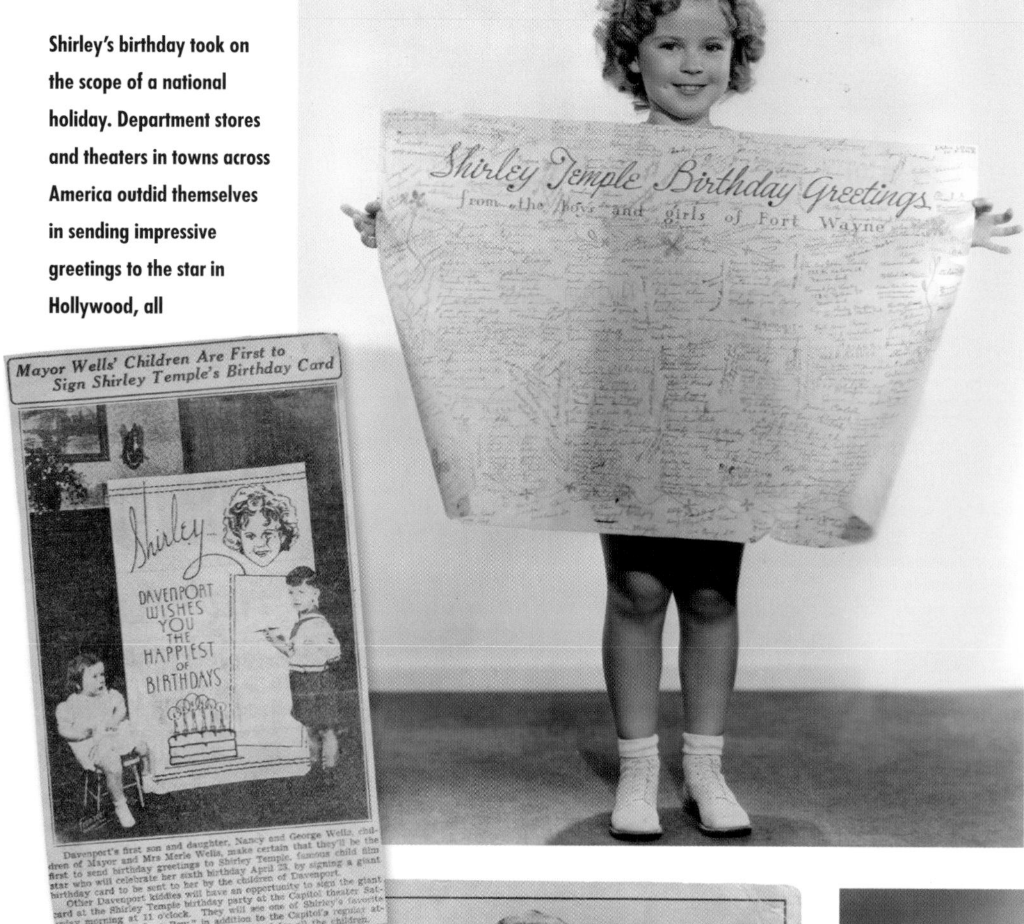


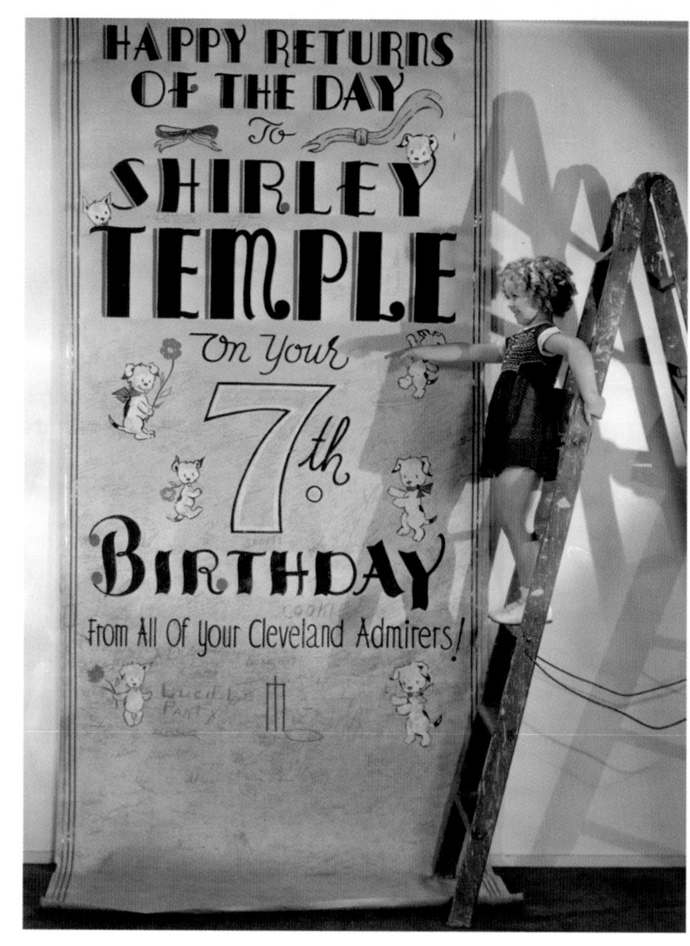

Bearing Loving Greetings for Your BIRTHDAY
Teddy and I are here to say-
May You be ever so Happy To-day
A Birthday Wish FOR A DEAR LITTLE GIRL!
A Great Big HAPPY BIRTHDAY
BIRTHDAY WISHES FOR TUESDAY
Racing to greet you with wishes sincere, For a jolly good time On Your Birthday my dear!
GREETINGS ON YOUR EIGHTH BIRTHDAY
Somebody's Eight Years Old To-day - And somebody wishes that somebody may Be ever so happy and bright and gay.
SHIRLEY TEMPLE
MANY HAPPY RETURNS!
BEARING GOOD WISHES FOR YOUR BIRTHDAY
8589 B.
SHIRLEY APR 23 A.M. 1938 VA.
SHIRLEY TEMPLE
So TUESDAY is Your BIRTHDAY
Little Shirley was born on TUESDAY— The dimpled prodigy
And so was Patrick Henry with his plea for Liberty
Roses for Love, and Forget-me-nots blue To show that I'm always Remembering You.

**Shirley's birthday celebration prompted a variety of ephemera, including an advertising card from Italy (below), an *Illustrated Current News* poster anticipating her upcoming "seventh" birthday (publicity stills were shot months in advance), magazine covers from almost every country around the world (this Danish *Ugebladet* issue dates from 1938), a card announcing a 1936 birthday event, Australian sheet music (this special song was issued in America also), a painted plaster cake topper and an unidentified box with artwork showing Shirley slicing a huge cake decorated with a Shirley Temple doll. Delicious!**

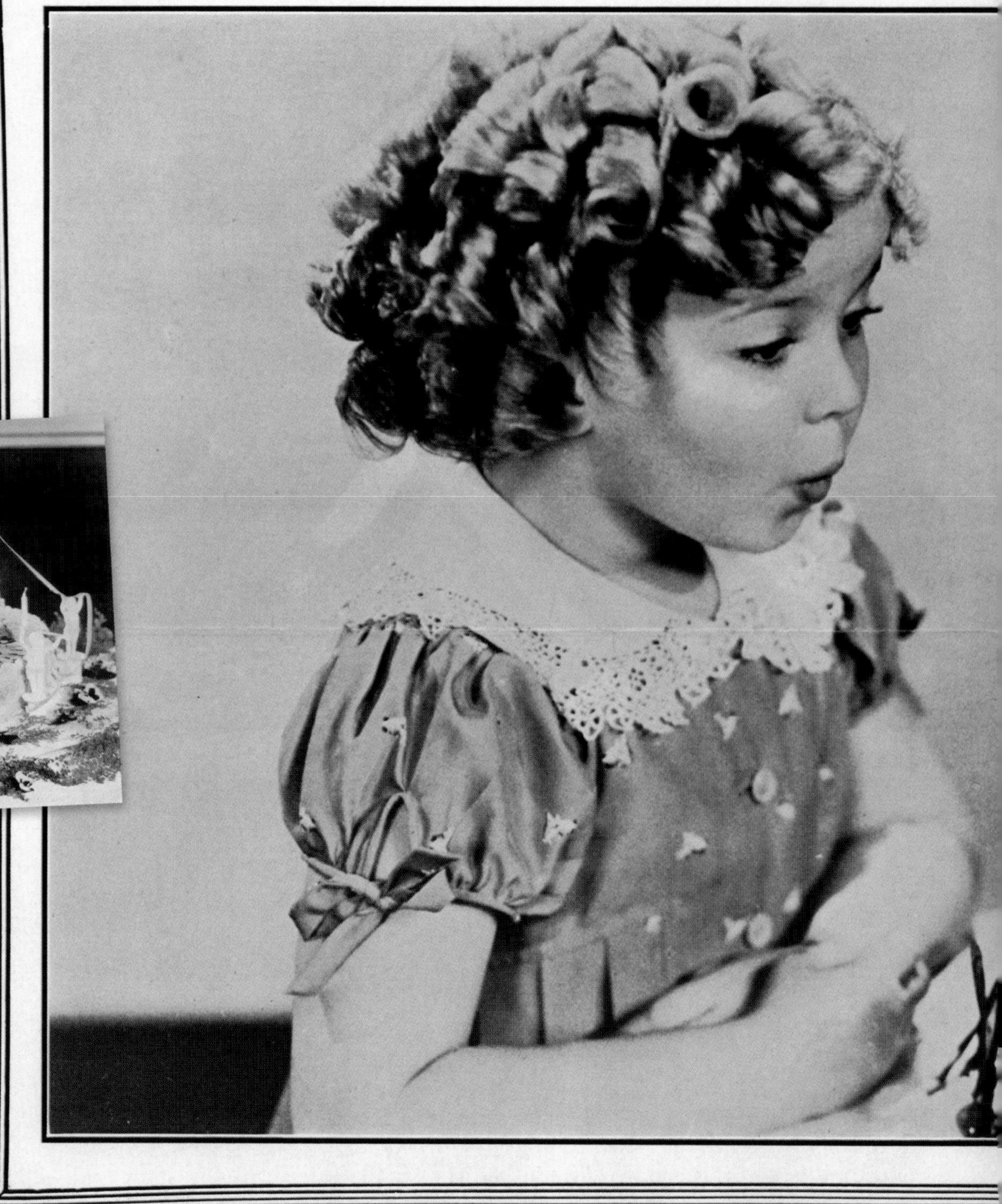

Entered as second-class matter April 15, 1931, at the post office at New Haven, Connecticut, under the act of March 3, 1879

ILLUSTRATE

"SOON

An actress to the core, Shirley Temple b
as birthday anniversaries. The child star is shown
for the big day, April 23rd.

CURRENT NEWS

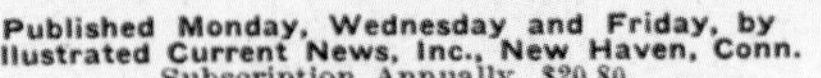
Published Monday, Wednesday and Friday, by
Illustrated Current News, Inc., New Haven, Conn.
Subscription Annually, $20.80

April 20, 1936—No. 3528

UGEBLADET
18 AARG. NO. 24
SØNDAG · 12 JUNI
HAPPY BIRTHDAY SHIRLEY
30 ØRE

VIL DE HAVE 25 KR.?
Følg med i vor Samlerkonkurrence

Celebrate With The Nation
SHIRLEY TEMPLE BIRTHDAY WEEK

Kiddies clubs, theatres and all retail outlets carrying Shirley Temple merchandise will participate in the celebration of her birthday, April 23rd. Music departments are urged to feature and display Shirley Temple songs during that week. Another opportunity to boost your sheet music sales!

From Shirley's Latest Picture "CAPTAIN JANUARY"
"THE RIGHT SOMEBODY TO LOVE"
"AT THE CODFISH BALL"
"EARLY BIRD"

Other Shirley Temple Hits:
"ANIMAL CRACKERS IN MY SOUP"
"POLLY WOLLY DOODLE"
"ON THE GOOD SHIP LOLLIPOP"
SHIRLEY TEMPLE SONG ALBUM

MOVIETONE MUSIC CORPORATION
SAM FOX PUBLISHING CO., Sole Agents

The Arcade
CLEVELAND, O.

1250 Sixth Ave.
(RCA Bldg. - Radio City)
NEW YORK, N. Y.

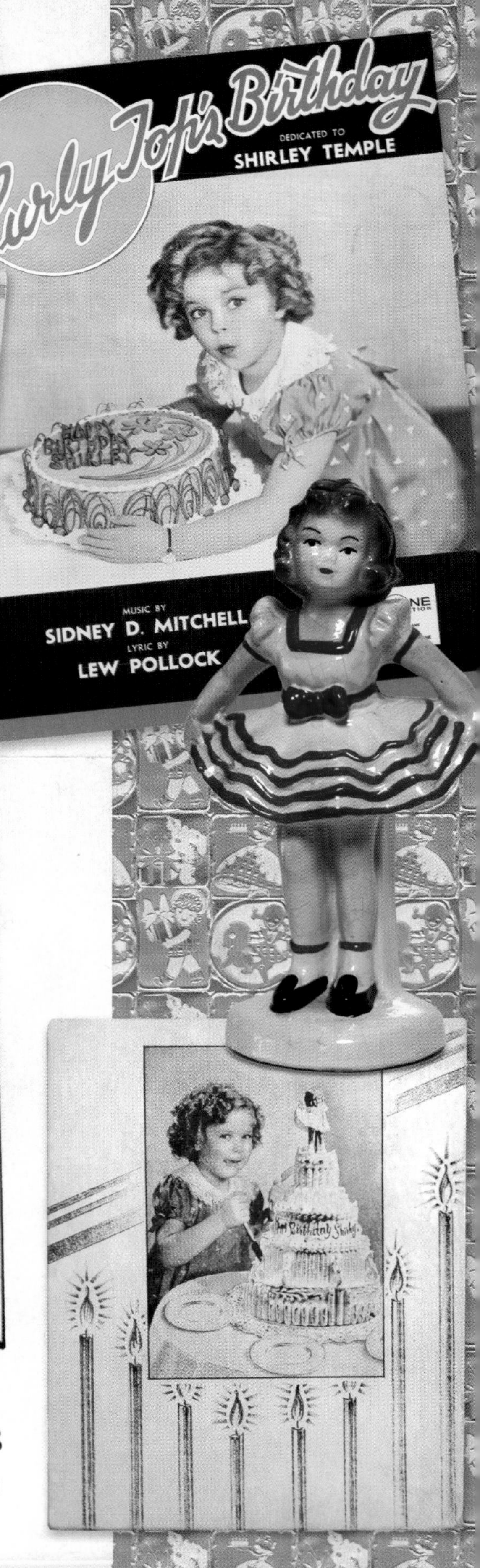


AM SEVEN"

ves in rehearsals even for such auspicious occasions nproving her "blowing out" technique in preparation

Shirley took part in other celebrations, too. These candid photos were preserved by Shirley's bodyguard, Grif, and show a Halloween party on the ***Rebecca of Sunnybrook Farm*** set and a cast birthday with the crew of ***Heidi***. When viewing Shirley's films today, one doesn't think about how young the crew responsible for all that screen magic was, and how they probably enjoyed any excuse to party. While the scope of the festivities were held down out of respect to Shirley's age, the crowd gathered around the young star look as if they're enjoying themselves. The photo at left shows Shirley's stand-in Mary Lou, as well as co-star Jean Hersholt and his stand-in. Bodyguard Grif stands at the far left, Mrs. Temple cuts one of the cakes at Shirley's right and teacher "Klammie" grins in a flowered dress at center right. The rest of the crew was the usual gathering of Shirley's studio pals. Bill Robinson appears in the ***Rebecca*** party photo, just above Shirley.

Above left: a 1937 Fox studio convention and an engraved silver cup that may have been a souvenir from that event. Left: An 11th birthday bash for comedian Harold Lloyd's daughter Gloria. Good friends for many years, Shirley was an honored guest at many of their childhood parties, as well as those given for Darryl Zanuck's daughters.

ROYAL HAWAIIAN HOTEL
Shirley's First Dinner Party
Shirley Temple
MATSON LINE
HONOLULU TO SAN FRANCISCO
SOUTH SEAS AND AUSTRALIA

Clockwise from top left: Shirley's first dinner party at the Royal Hawaiian Hotel in 1937, an impromptu ukulele serenade during the same trip, posing with another visitor in 1935, a souvenir photo from the Schofield Barracks and welcoming crowds at the Matson Cruise Lines dock in 1937. Below: Grinning along with Olympic surfing legend Duke Kahanamoku in 1935.

# "Shirley Temple is Coming to Town!"

"Oh Mom, I wanna see Shirley!" The title of a *Photoplay* magazine column feature reflected the reaction of the kids of America when learning that Shirley and the Temples were planning an excursion to see America in 1938. Mrs. Temple was determined to keep Shirley's environment as normal as possible; including family vacations like any other kid—only the family expanded to include a support entourage as well.

Hawaii was also a favorite spot for the Temples, traveling there three times during Shirley's childhood. Their first trip was shortly after Shirley became a household name in 1935—ten thousand people turned out at the Matson Line dock in Honolulu to greet Shirley's ship as it arrived. The massive but friendly crowd shocked the Temples, who escaped through a private exit instead of parading down the gangplank. To make up for the crowd's inability to see their idol, Shirley made a special appearance at the Iolani Royal Palace to sing

"On the Good Ship Lollipop" to thousands of gathered fans. The adulation never ceased on any of Shirley's trips to the Islands. She was showered with gifts, given special dinner parties at the Royal Hawaiian Hotel and escorted by Olympic surfing legend Duke Kahanamoku. She visited Pearl Harbor, was the guest of honor at a children's party held for her by the Fagins (the family who was first to promote tourist trade for the Islands) and given special tours of attractions such as the Dole Pineapple plant. Most of all, she wanted to see a volcano erupt. Shirley adored Hawaii; in 1950, she met her husband Charles Black there.

In 1938, the Temples planned a cross-country auto trip—"a junket to educate me," as teenage Shirley recalled in *My Young Life*. Stops included Pike's Peak, Utah, Kansas, Chicago, Washington D.C. (where she met with President Roosevelt), New York and Boston, with a side trip to Bermuda. Sickness in Boston kept her in bed for a few days and put the country into a panic. When she recovered, 5000 people turned out to watch her ride a swan boat on Boston Commons. Mrs. Temple never planned the trip as a promotional tour, in fact, she turned down fabulous offers for personal appearances. If fans saw Shirley along the way, it was fine—"Shirley belongs to the children," Mrs. Temple remarked in one interview.

Other childhood excursions included motoring to Vancouver and regular trips to Palm Springs for well-deserved relaxation between films.

**Clockwise from top left: A ride on a speedboat at Pearl Harbor with Dad and Grif in 1937, a page taken from an album made by a friend of the Fagin family documenting a garden party thrown for Shirley in August 1937, a 1935 visit with a young patient at the Shriner's hospital in Honolulu, Shirley and her honorary Waikiki Beach surfboard with Captain Bergmann of the S.S. Matsonia in 1935, a group "aloha" photo of Shirley and her parents in 1939, inspecting pineapples in 1937 and on board the Matson Line to Hawaii in 1935. Bottom: A 1938 Saalfield children's book containing Shirley's "own Honolulu diary."**

HELÉNE'S
Party
FOR
Shirley Temple
Shirley Temple visits our Honolulu Hospital and is presented with the traditional "Lei."
The occasion of Shirley Temple's visit to the Hospital was a real "red letter" day to the children and one which will always be remembered. Shirley sang the "Lollipop Song" for them, accompanied by one of our little fellows on his guitar. The song was sung by all ages and nationalities—in some instances almost unrecognizable—for many months after.
19
ALOHA
Capt. Shirley
THOUSANDS ON HAND TO GREET SHIRLEY TEMPLE, HERE FOR 3 WEEK STAY

HONOLULU STAR-BULLETIN, MONDAY, JULY 29, 1935

# SHIRLEY TEMPLE'S CONQUEST OF HONOLULU ON ARRIVAL TODAY

Honolulu Star-Bulletin LAST EDITION

FDR THREATENS SUGAR BILL VETO

15,000 Greet 'Queen' Shirley

SUBJECTS OLD, YOUNG, CROWD PIER, STREETS

GOVERNOR TO SEEK U. S. AID OF $1,894,614

Textbooks Will Be Discarded At Whittier College

IS OPPOSED TO LEGISLATION IN PRESENT FORM

MAHOE HANGS, UNTOUCHED BY FEAR, REMORSE

AMERICANS IN CHINA WARNED OF WAR PERIL

America's Cup To Stay In U.S.; Ranger Again Victor

BALCH RETIRES FROM SEAT ON HOMES BOARD

Pork Extension Bill Charged By Group In Senate

BASEBALL

LATE SPORTS

Sugar Bill A Repudiation Of Promises, Says King

MANY PHONE CALLS

Letter Drafted To Mrs. Cromwell

Capt. Friedell Arrives For Duty

1 2 3 4 5

These photos were among many taken this morning as moviedom's most famous little actress came to Honolulu for a vacation. 1—A portion of the 10,000 persons who jammed Pier 11 to catch a glimpse of Shirley before she and her parents were whisked away from the boat to their hotel. 2—Shirley is seen waving a cheery salute to Capt. William R. Meyer of the Mariposa. 3—From left to right: Shirley's father, George Temple, Shirley and Shirley's mother. 4—Honolulu's famous citizen, Sheriff Duke Kahanamoku, extends the city's official greetings to the little star and to Christine, her flaming haired doll. 5—Shirley is greeted by six-year-old Jerry Lee Culver. —Star-Bulletin photos. Kahanamoku-Temple photo by Mid-Pacific Press Bureau.

**Public life, private life—Shirley as newsmaker in Hawaii, above. At right: Shirley gives ukulele lessons to local pals in front of the home she and her family stayed in during her 1939 visit.**

Shirley sings in front of thousands of fans at the Iolani Royal Palace in 1935.

The larger-than-life-size bride doll at left was a gift from Japanese schoolchildren. The figure was so lifelike that it terrified Mrs. Temple and Shirley when they first encountered it in their hotel room. Below: Shirley and Christine, her traveling companion in 1935.

Opposite: Souvenirs from various trips to Hawaii include menus from the Royal Hawaiian Hotel and the Matson Lines, as well as snapshots from the beach and Pearl Harbor.

Dinner

*tendered to*

Mrs. George Temple

Mr. George Temple

Mrs. John V. Griffith

Mr. John B. Griffith

Mr. Charles D. Raudebaugh

*and*

Miss Shirley Temple

Aboard S. S. Malolo

*Enroute to California*

*Monday, August 23, 1937*

Shirley's 1936 visit to Vancouver included a stop at Mt. Ranier in Washington State. The snapshot at left shows Shirley as she appeared in between films, without a dental cap used to hide the space made by a missing baby tooth. Inset: Shirley confers with a chipmunk at Ranier National Park.

Opposite: Activities in Vancouver included fishing and lunching with Dad. A petty cash receipt for the tour was retained by Shirley's bodyguard, Grif.

Received from John Griffith $1,148.71 and
miscellaneous statements in connection with
Shirley Temple trip.
Cecile Farrell
Mr. Metzler's Office
8-17-36.
The
ISLAND MOTORIST
and
Georgian
Circuit
Magazine
The Only
International
Auto-Tourist
Magazine
in the
World
Photo, Courtesy
Associated
Screen News
Engraving Courtesy
Victoria Daily Times
SHIRLEY TEMPLE IN A NEW ROLE
CATCH AT BRENTWOOD, VICTORIA, B. C.
SHIRLEY TEMPLE
PHOTOGRAPHED WITH THE CHINESE TROUPERS.
CHINESE CARNIVAL.

Shirley gave these autographed cards out to kids along the way.

A boat trip around New York Harbor.

Home movies on the Capitol steps.

Panda at the Brookfield Zoo in Chicago.

Back to California by train.

A gift from Utah.

At the White House.

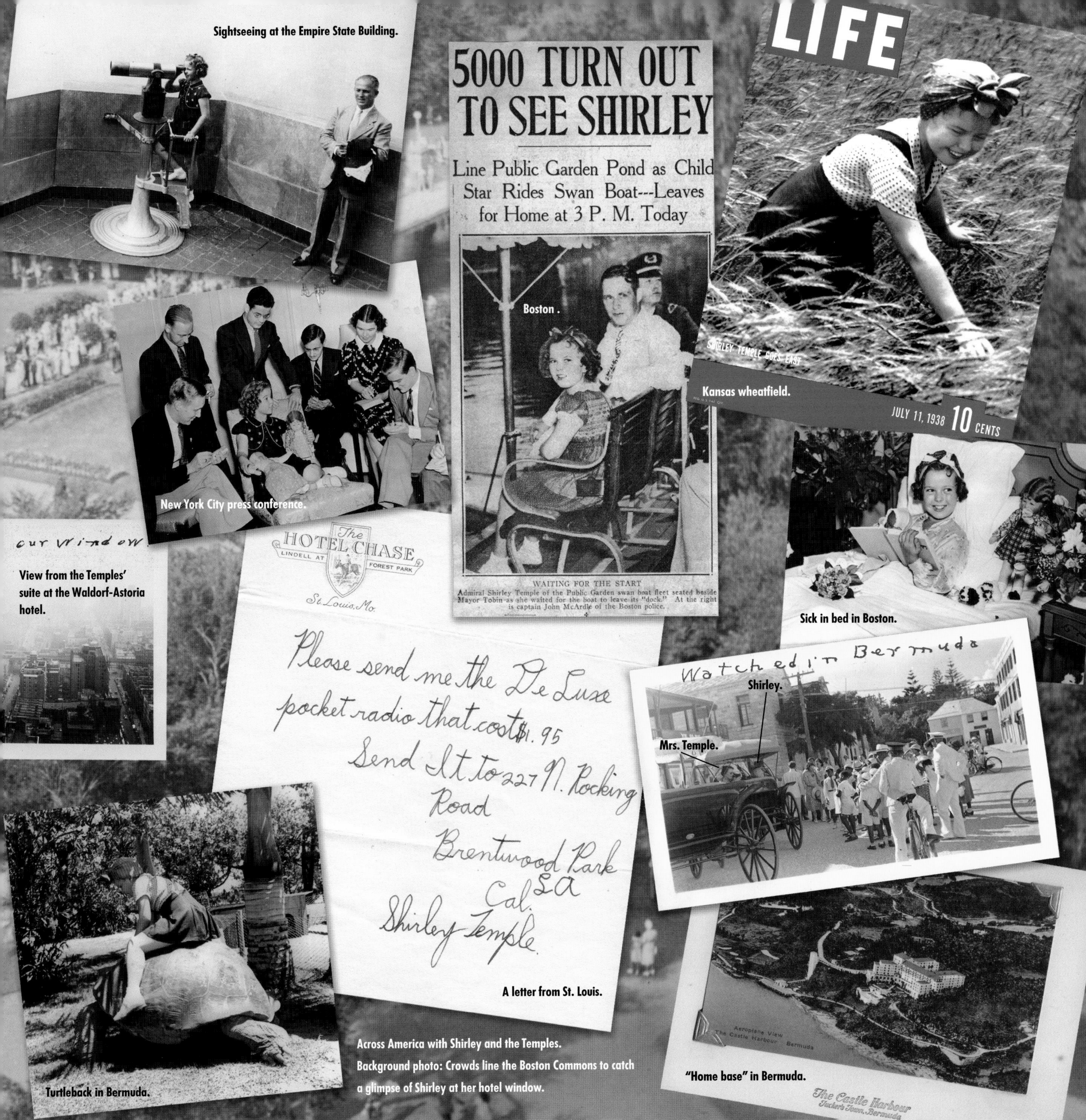

5000 TURN OUT TO SEE SHIRLEY
Line Public Garden Pond as Child Star Rides Swan Boat---Leaves for Home at 3 P. M. Today
WAITING FOR THE START
Admiral Shirley Temple of the Public Garden swan boat fleet seated beside Mayor Tobin as she waited for the boat to leave its "dock." At the right is captain John McArdle of the Boston police.
LIFE
SHIRLEY TEMPLE GOES EAST
JULY 11, 1938 10 CENTS
our Window
The HOTEL CHASE
LINDELL AT FOREST PARK
St. Louis, Mo.
Please send me the De Luxe
pocket radio that cost $1.95
Send It to 227 N. Rocking
Road
Brentwood Park
LA
Cal.
Shirley Temple
Watched in Bermuda
Aeroplane View
The Castle Harbour Bermuda
The Castle Harbour
Tucker's Town, Bermuda


Sightseeing at the Empire State Building.

New York City press conference.

Boston.

Kansas wheatfield.

Sick in bed in Boston.

View from the Temples' suite at the Waldorf-Astoria hotel.

Shirley.

Mrs. Temple.

A letter from St. Louis.

Turtleback in Bermuda.

"Home base" in Bermuda.

Across America with Shirley and the Temples. Background photo: Crowds line the Boston Commons to catch a glimpse of Shirley at her hotel window.

OUTDOORS and IN
November, 1938

DESERT INN-SEPARABLES

Smash! A bottle of milk christens the "Shirley Temple Bungalow" on the Desert Inn grounds, Palm Springs . . . and who else should christen it but she whom it was built for, named for, and whose vacations it is dedicated to . . . Shirley Temple! Indulgently Mrs. Nellie N. Coffman, gracious Desert Inn managing owner, smiles at her favorite guest.



Sun and fun in Palm Springs. Shirley with pet pup Corky (far left) and with her mom (below left). At right: Shirley reads the comics—*Tarzan* was her favorite. Opposite: a cowboy themed party in 1937, and an Easter fest in 1938.

Easter Party

明けまして
おめでたう
元旦
Shirley
ALBUM N2
ALBUM DI DISEGNI PER
CONTIENE FUORI TESTO
EDIZIONI
"DE KLEINE
KOLONEL"
SHIRLEY TEMPLE
ΘΕΑΤΗΣ
192
Ф-ка „Ерди"
Шарлей Темплъ
SHIRLEY
in
"CURLY TOP"
FOX FILM

# Ambassadorette

"What? No more worlds for Shirley to conquer?" asked a 1936 movie magazine that printed the photograph from *Dimples* on the opposite page. Shirley *had* conquered the planet—keepsakes reached epic proportions abroad as manufacturers scrambled to take advantage of Shirley's popularity. Shirley was a hit in England, France, Italy, Spain, Central America, Japan, Poland, Australia, Czechoslovakia, China, India, Palestine, South Africa, Latvia—she was instantly recognized in all corners of the globe. Most of the items produced outside America were unauthorized, with the bulk of these mementoes originating in Japan. Shirley was as popular there as she was in the States: the press reported that one magazine produced a single Shirley Temple issue with no text, just a gallery of photographs—and immediately sold thousands of copies. At the height of her career, Shirley made a special recording of traditional children's songs for her fans in Japan, singing phonetically in their language.

Magazines, books, figures, toys, household items—Shirley was found everywhere. A trade card from Palestine had text in Hebrew; a post-war advertising card promoting Esperanto, the universal language, used Shirley as the representation of an American child (below). A biscuit tin from Australia used a scene from *Curly Top*. Posters and ads heralded the release of Shirley's films,

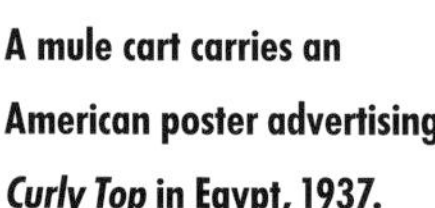
**A mule cart carries an American poster advertising *Curly Top* in Egypt, 1937.**

just as in the United States. People corresponded by mail using Shirley Temple postcards, which numbered in the thousands. Kids kept Shirley Temple scrapbooks and swapped Shirley Temple gum cards. Shirley's picture adorned matchboxes, as well as hand fans and poster stamps. With no color reference available, many of the portraits showed Shirley as a stereotypical blonde-haired and often very blue-eyed child, contrasting with her true brown-eyed coloring.

Most intriguing, though, is a calendar book from Czechoslovakia that used a jester-like character named Humorek who traveled the world over the year. July's "trip" to America was represented by Hollywood, where he met the world's most recognizable icons of the screen—Chaplin, Garbo, Laurel and Hardy, Mickey Mouse—and Shirley.

Shirley Temple
FOX FILM STAR
FOX
SHIRLEY TEMPLE
ČERVENEC
V červenci lze zahnat nudu
stoprocentně v Holywúdu,
věřte tomu – lidičky –
Humorek si aspoň chválí,
jak jej vřele uvítaly
holywúdské hvězdičky!
Amerika – zázrak světa
nač si vzpomeneš, vše tu zk
v zlato mění se i koks;
bují tady jazz-band, káv
filmová jepičí sláva,
gangstři, cowboyky i bo
CASA EDITRICE
CARROCCIO
MILANO
BRE NIÑA RICA"
RAISO de los NIÑOS - Sarandí 620

テムプルちやんと
日本のお嬢さん達
REGISTERED TRADE MARK
POLYFAR POLYDOR RECORDING
POLYDOR
2409
(日本語)
Yuyake Koyake (Kusagawa) (夕焼小焼)
Kutsu ga naru (R. Hirota) (靴が鳴る)
Omocha no March (Odajima) (玩具のマーチ)
Sudzume no Gakko (R. Hirota)
Shirley Temple
(Dtsch) mit Orchester
MANUFACTURED BY NIPPON POLYDOR CHIKUONKI CO., LTD., TOKIO, JAPAN.
納付済
テンプルの童謠
Shirley TEMPLE in Dimples
ポリドール POLYDOR レコード

皆さんと、おなじみのアメリカの人氣者……子役俳優のシャーリー・テムプルちゃんは日本の皆さんとも、お友達になりたがつてゐます。

先日、アメリカの學校にゐる日本のお嬢さんたちを二人の先生と一緒に、綺麗なテムプルちゃんのお家へ招待して賑やかな晩餐會を開きました。

美しい振袖の着物で勢揃ひした日本のお嬢さんたちは、お招ばれのお禮に、綺麗な日本のお人形を、テムプルちゃんにプレゼントしました。

テムプルちゃんは大變よろこんで、日本にゐるお嬢さんたちにも「よろしく言つて頂戴ね」との、お傳言でありました。

Above: Shirley hosts a party for visiting Japanese schoolgirls. Right: A collage figure taken from a Japanese postcard. Opposite: The only known example of Shirley singing in a language other than English: a 1936 recording of traditional children's songs made for distribution in Japan.

In 1935, *Screen Pictorial* of Japan published this special magazine using only photos of Shirley with no text, and sold out the edition as soon as it hit the stands.

Opposite: A wide range of books and publications with Shirley as the theme, published in Spain, Holland, Denmark, Italy, Australia, France and Sweden. The small illustration at the top is taken from the Italian children's biography *Aneddoti e Vita di Shirley Temple*, shown at the lower right.

SHIRLEY TEMPLE
SA VIE SES FILMS
N°. 6
36 PAGES
2 FRANCS
PUBLICATION MENSUELLE ILLUSTRÉE PAR DE NOMBREUSES PHOTOGRAPHIES
EN SUPPLÉMENT UN MAGNIFIQUE PORTRAIT HORS TEXTE
VECKO-REVYNS KUPONGBOK
SHIRLEY TEMPLES SAGA
ÅHLÉN & ÅKERLUNDS FÖRLAG
BIBLIOTHÈQUE ROSE
SUSANNAH DE LA POLICE MONTÉE
(SHIRLEY TEMPLE)
HACHETTE
VINCENZO BAGGIOLI
Shirley Temple
la reginetta del cinema
25 fotografie
NERBINI EDITORE-FIRENZE
Shirley Temple
EIN KIND GEHT ZUM FILM
SHIRLEY TEMPLE'S ANNUAL

The WORLD'S Little Sweetheart
SHIRLEY TEMPLE

THE STORY OF MY LIFE BY SHIRLEY TEMPLE
Shirley Temple
BIBLIOTECA PER TUTTI
NONNO EBE
ANEDDOTI E VITA DI SHIRLEY TEMPLE
SHIRLEY TEMPLE
MIN EGEN DAGBOG
LA PICCOLA GRANDE ATTRICE DELLO SCHERMO
SHIRLEY TEMPLE
(20th CENTURY FOX)

China figurines from Europe captured Shirley's essence—and movie costumes—perfectly.

Opposite: A brown-haired, brown eyed wall mask by Goldscheider of Austria.

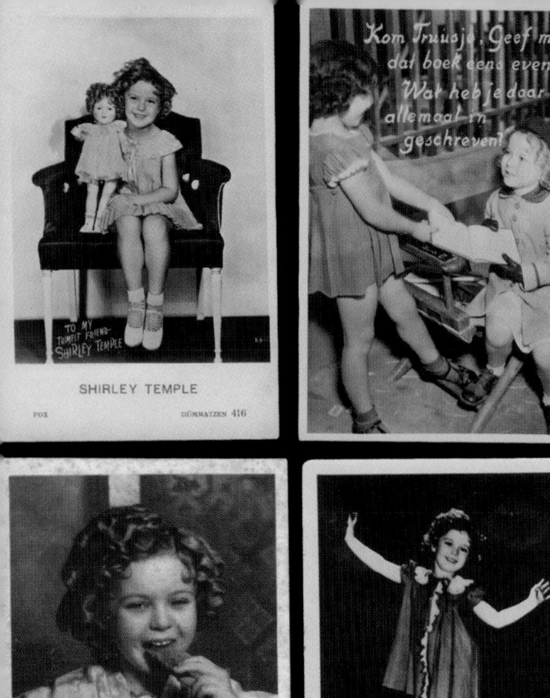
TO MY TRUSTY FRIEND—
SHIRLEY TEMPLE
SHIRLEY TEMPLE
FOX
DÜMMATZEN 416
Kom Truusje, Geef mij
dat boek eens even
Wat heb je daar
allemaal in
geschreven?

Fox Film
Shirley Temple

SHIRLEY TEMPLE
(Fox)

Muchas
Felicidades
SHIRLEY TEMPLE - 20th CENTURY - FOX

Tenemos un angelito que tiene mucho apetito.

Mano draugams
SHIRLEY TEMPLE

SHIRLEY TEMPLE DANS « LA FILLE DU REBELLE ».

Daudz laimes
vārda dienā!

Shirley
Temple

Ширлей Темпль

新年おめでとう
ございます
一月一日
I love
Shirley Temple

Fox film
Shirley Temple
659

SHIRLEY TEMPLE

Shirley Temple

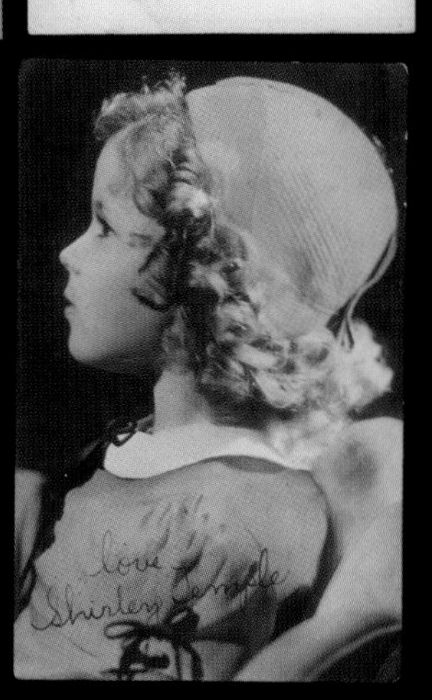
love
Shirley Temple

SHIRLEY TEMPLE, MOTOCYCLISTE.

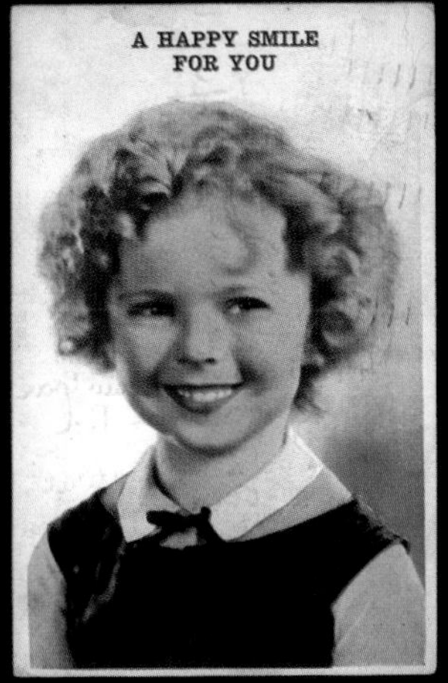

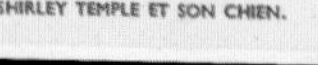

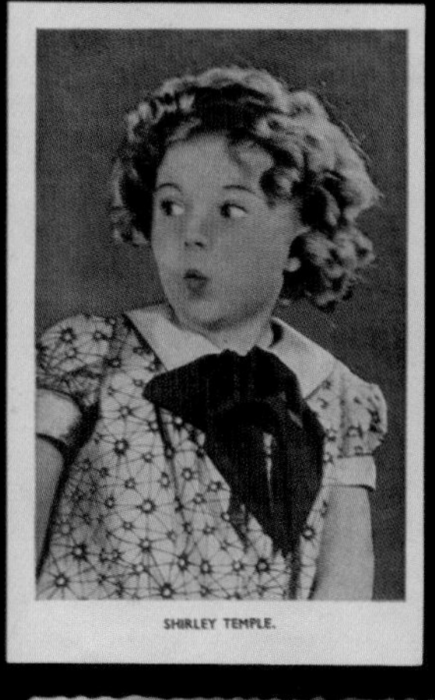

Me resulta un navegante
un poco "tirao pa alante"

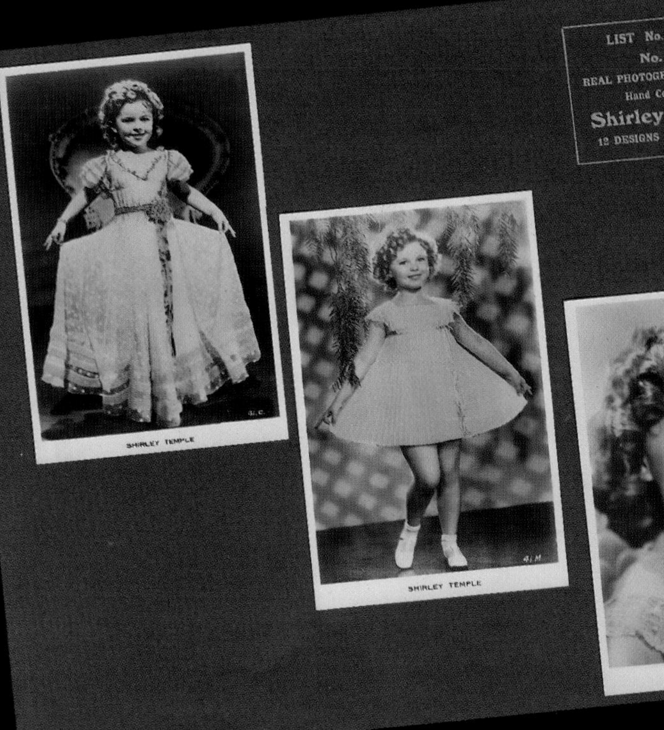

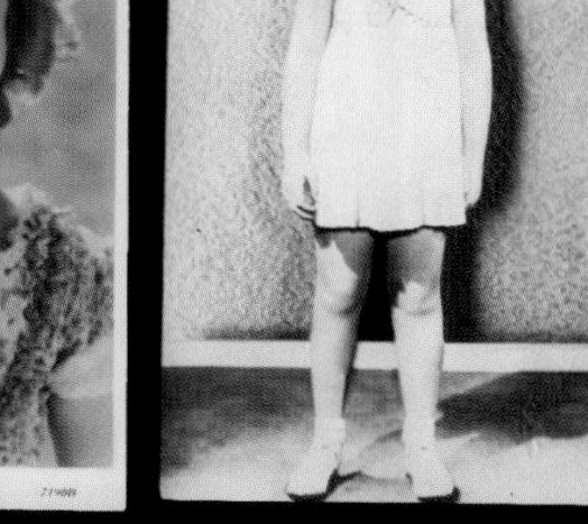

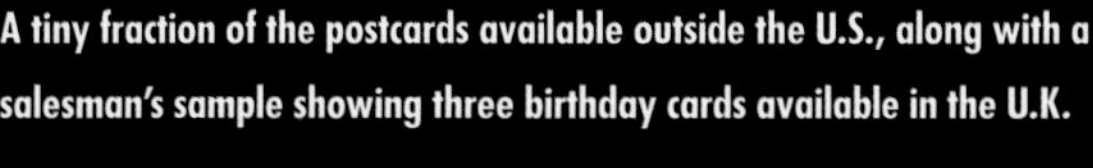

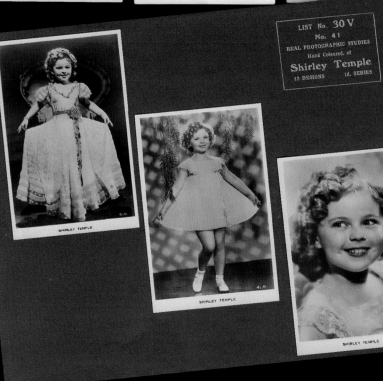

A tiny fraction of the postcards available outside the U.S., along with a salesman's sample showing three birthday cards available in the U.K.

SHIRLEY TEMPLE—THE DAINTY YOUNG 20TH CENTURY FOX STAR.

WITH COMPLIMENTS FROM

K. CHAMBERS

Art Needlework Specialist

3, Greenmarket & 11, Lowther Street, Carlisle

JANUARY 1937

| SUN | MON | TUE | WED | THUR | FRI | SAT |
|---|---|---|---|---|---|---|
| ☾ 4th. | ● 12th. | ☽ 19th | ○ 26th | ◊ | 1 | 2 |
| 3 | 4 | 5 | 6 | 7 | 8 | 9 |
| 10 | 11 | 12 | 13 | 14 | 15 | 16 |
| 17 | 18 | 19 | 20 | 21 | 22 | 23 |
| 24/31 | 25 | 26 | 27 | 28 | 29 | 30 |

Calendars from England (left), Italy (below), Spain (right), and Japan (bottom right). The small calendar booklet at the top right was an Italian barber shop giveaway.

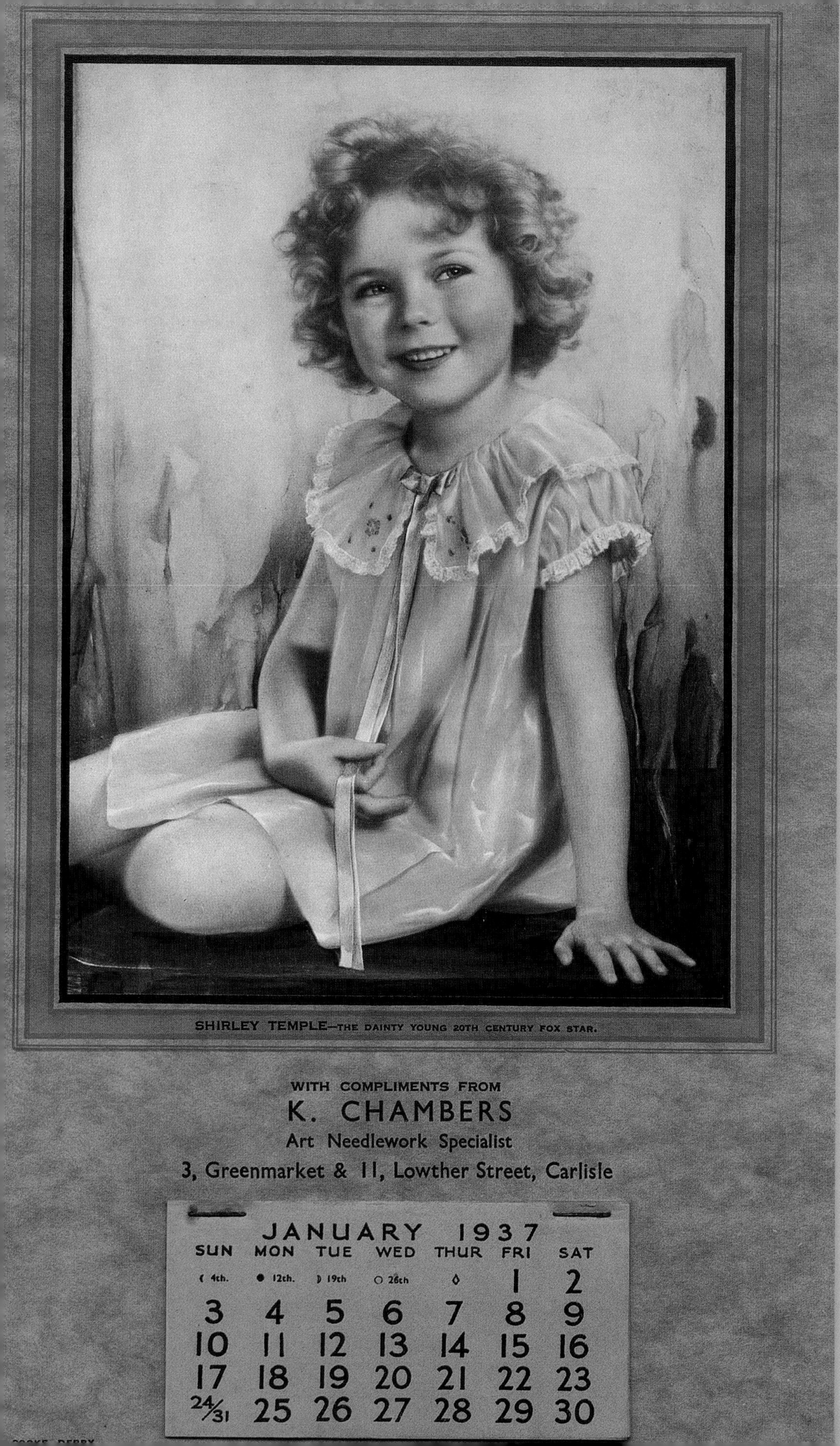

100

| 1938 | | | ENERO | | | 1938 |
|---|---|---|---|---|---|---|
| | 1 - Año Nuevo | | 6 - Dia de los niños | | | |
| Domingo | Lunes | Martes | Miér. | Jueves | Viernes | Sábado |
| | | | | | | 1 |
| 2 | 3 | 4 | 5 | 6 | 7 | 8 |
| 9 | 10 | 11 | 12 | 13 | 14 | 15 |
| 16 | 17 | 18 | 19 | 20 | 21 | 22 |
| 23/30 | 24/31 | 25 | 26 | 27 | 28 | 29 |

1937
FARMACIA
DEL
BEATO ANGELO
CUNEO
Corso Nizza 48 - Telef. 4.16
Dott. Prof. M. Rossi Nicodemi
FARMACISTA
OMAGGIO
Calendario
del cinema
anno 1937-XV.
Sia per voi
anno
propizio

SHIRLEY TEMPLE

OCT. 1936

| Sun | Mon | Tue | Wed | Thu | Fri | Sat |
|---|---|---|---|---|---|---|
| ... | ... | ... | ... | 1 | 2 | 3 |
| 4 | 5 | 6 | 7 | 8 | 9 | 10 |
| 11 | 12 | 13 | 14 | 15 | 16 | 17 |
| 18 | 19 | 20 | 21 | 22 | 23 | 24 |
| 25 | 26 | 27 | 28 | 29 | 30 | 31 |

NOV. 1936

| Sun | Mon | Tue | Wed | Thu | Fri | Sat |
|---|---|---|---|---|---|---|
| 1 | 2 | 3 | 4 | 5 | 6 | 7 |
| 8 | 9 | 10 | 11 | 12 | 13 | 14 |
| 15 | 16 | 17 | 18 | 19 | 20 | 21 |
| 22 | 23 | 24 | 25 | 26 | 27 | 28 |
| 29 | 30 | ... | ... | ... | ... | ... |

THE EIGA NO TOMO CALENDAR: The Eiga Sekai Publishing Co.

SHIRLEY TEMPLE
FOX STAR
A DELIGHTFUL
SHIRLEY TEMPLE
BOX OF CHOCOLATES
IS OFFERED TO PURCHASERS OF
CARR'S BISCUITS
OR PARTICULARS OF KINDS OF BISCUITS TO BE PURCHASED
D CLAIM THIS LOVELY BOX OF CHOCOLATES.
CLOSING DATE SEPTEMBER 30th, 1936.
Shirley Temple
FOX FILMS
48
Elit
Çikolatasi
Shirley Temple
57
Elit
Çikolatasi
Shirley Temple

**Confections and Shirley were a natural combination—a Carr's Biscuit poster advertises a box of Shirley chocolates, at left. Also shown: A British cake tin with a serious pose and two chocolate cards from Turkey.**

A café poster from Italy advertises hazelnut-filled wafers.

Printed in Germany
1687

Various cards and German "relief scraps"—tiny figures used to trim packages and valentines.

SHIRLEY TEMPLE
Fox Star
No. 10 of a SET. IMPORTANT, see other side.

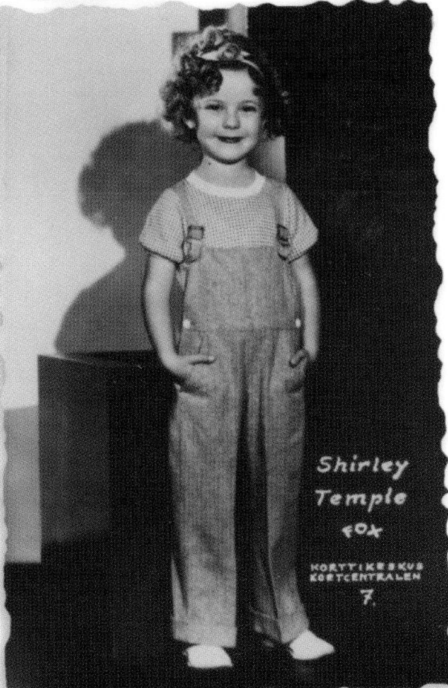

Celluloid figures from Japan, a boxed jigsaw puzzle from Holland and a metal statuette from Argentina.

A fan with rolling eyes, a wooden jewelry box, a spool doll, a Chinese powder box and a post-war European metal bank—made as a souvenir and brought back to the States by an American soldier.

Pinback buttons and brooches from around the world in a variety of materials including plastic, Bakelite, tin and glass.

Opposite: An elaborate enameled coat button from India.

SHIRLEY TEMPLE
En CHEWING GUM toutes présentations
EXIGEZ de votre FOURNISSEUR toujours " MARBETT", le meilleur, le plus fin, le mieux parfumé
VAL Chewing Gum
Shirley Temple ALBUM


A large series of cards issued in pre-war packs of Val Gum were popular for swapping and gluing into specially made albums.

218 SHIRLEY TEMPLE

PRINTED IN HOLLAND
216 SHIRLEY TEMPLE

PRINTED IN HOLLAND
217 SHIRLEY TEMPLE

PRINTED IN HOLLAND
212 SHIRLEY TEMPLE

PRINTED IN HOLLAND
157 SHIRLEY TEMPLE

PRINTED IN HOLLAND
137 SHIRLEY TEMPLE

102 SHIRLEY TEMPLE

PRINTED IN HOLLAND
225 SHIRLEY TEMPLE

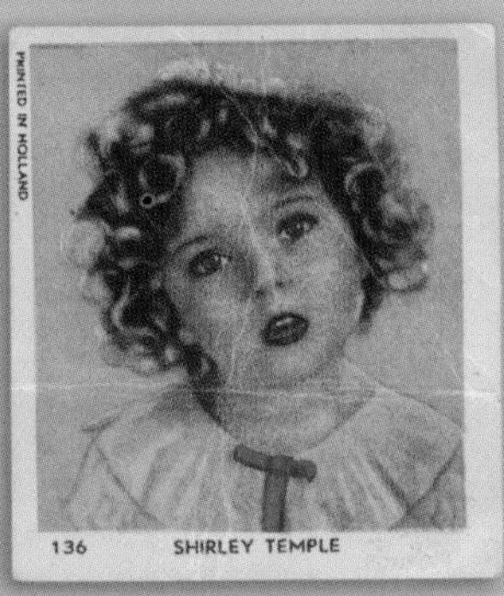
PRINTED IN HOLLAND
136 SHIRLEY TEMPLE

234 SHIRLEY TEMPLE

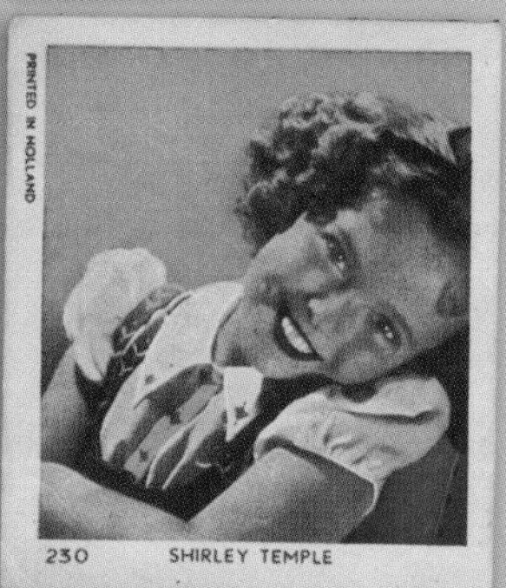
PRINTED IN HOLLAND
230 SHIRLEY TEMPLE

PRINTED IN HOLLAND
119 SHIRLEY TEMPLE

25 SHIRLEY TEMPLE

PRINTED IN HOLLAND
219 SHIRLEY TEMPLE

PRINTED IN HOLLAND
229 SHIRLEY TEMPLE

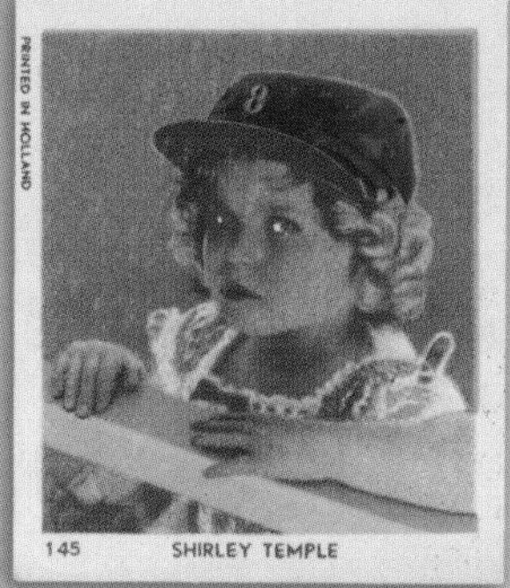
PRINTED IN HOLLAND
145 SHIRLEY TEMPLE

PRINTED IN HOLLAND
237 SHIRLEY TEMPLE

PRINTED IN HOLLAND
153 SHIRLEY TEMPLE

221 SHIRLEY TEMPLE

PRINTED IN HOLLAND
112 SHIRLEY TEMPLE

PRINTED IN HOLLAND
109 SHIRLEY TEMPLE

PRINTED IN HOLLAND
135 SHIRLEY TEMPLE

PRINTED IN HOLLAND
127 SHIRLEY TEMPLE

PRINTED IN HOLLAND
115 SHIRLEY TEMPLE

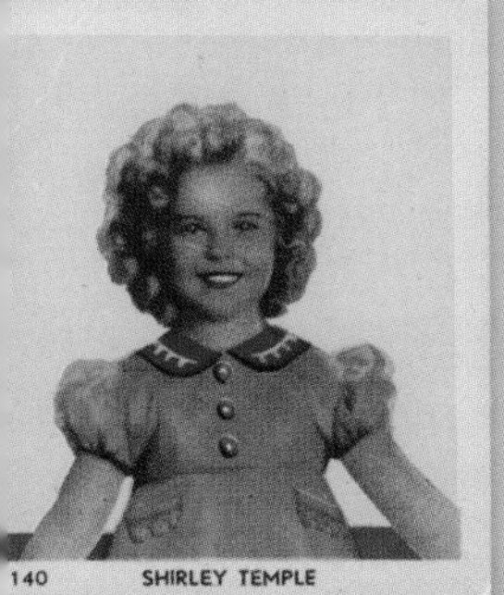
140 SHIRLEY TEMPLE

PRINTED IN HOLLAND
240 SHIRLEY TEMPLE

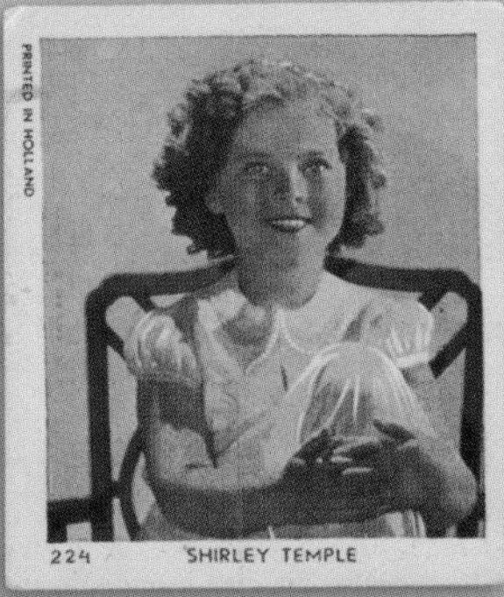
PRINTED IN HOLLAND
224 SHIRLEY TEMPLE

PRINTED IN HOLLAND
128 SHIRLEY TEMPLE

PRINTED IN HOLLAND
113 SHIRLEY TEMPLE

PRINTED IN HOLLAND
120 SHIRLEY TEMPLE

秀蘭鄧波兒版
No.1057
Szinházi Élet
SZERKESZTI
INCZE SÁNDOR
ANGELO COLOR
Kezdődik az iskola!
SHIRLEY TEMPLE
1938. 38 sz.
25 CENT
Shirley Temple
FOX STAR
TOMMY
e Jenny
2 vel + 1 enveloppe
nog geen 5 gram
SHIRLEY-TEMPLE-BLOC
Geka
100 vel met de pen
beschrijfbaar Luchtmailpapier

MARIE VOŘÍŠKOVÁ
HVĚZDA NA SLUNEČNÉM RANČI
...
MAMIČKO, VRAŤ SE!

**Back to school around the world, armed with writing tablets, bookmarks, an Italian reading book using an illustration of Shirley on the front and a Chinese book cover showing Shirley and an Afghan hound from *Just Around the Corner*.**

**Overleaf: International magazines featuring Shirley on the cover numbered in the hundreds.**

FiT
35 CENT
SPORT-Leven-AVONTUUR
HUSFRUE
GLÆDELIGT NYTAAR
PROYECTOR
MAGAZINE ESPAÑOL DE CINE
GODFREY WINN'S SATURDAY PAGE : SHIRLEY TEMPLE'S LIFE STORY
Woman's Illustrated
2d
Woman's Illustrated

ANNO IV - N° 21 - 1 NOVEMBRE 1936-XV
SHIRLEY TEMPLE
(FOX)

cine romanzo

UGEBLADET
SHIRLEY TEMPLE
Klostret, ingen Kvinder maa betræde
Hela Världen
Nr 34
15 öre

Rose France
Le Journal de la Française

POPULAR MUSIC
COMBINED WITH SHOWS
DECEMBER 28, 1935
MERRY XMAS TO EVERYBODY
SHIRLEY TEMPLE

THE NEW ID
SHIRLEY TEMPLE
CHILDREN OF THE ROYAL FA
An Exclusive Article

PHOTOPLAYER
TALKIES
SHIRLEY TEMPLE
DEARBORN FACE POWDER
Le Matin
MinervA

CINEGRAF

BUDGET
3D
CINEARTE
Shirley Temple

fémina

FON FON
Molde no Supplemento

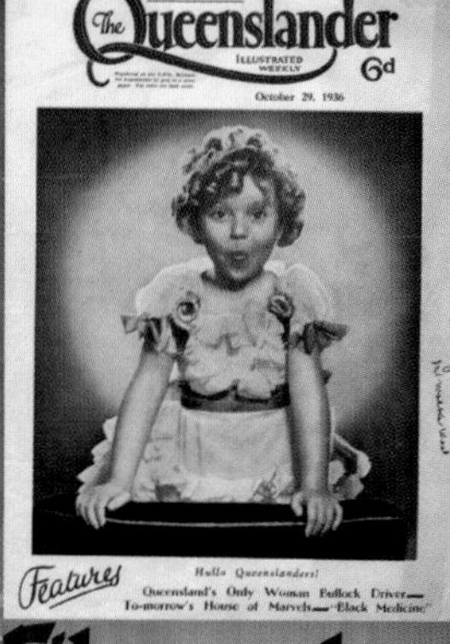
Frogs for Lunch!
The Queenslander
ILLUSTRATED WEEKLY
6d
October 29, 1936
Hullo Queenslanders!
Features

Allas
15 ÖRE
Nº 16
Veckotidning

Hemmets Veckotidning
Nº 4
25 öre
alba
SETTIMANALE FEMMINILE
CENT 30

The AUSTRALASIAN
PICTORIAL

Çocuk Sesi
5 Kr

Filmwoche
Die illustrierte
mit Photo-Teil
30

SINFONIA
SHIRLEY TEMPLE

VEA

FILMLAND'S GREATEST ROMANCE
PICTUREGOER
2d
WEEKLY

8me ANNÉE
Nº 326
4 MARS 1938
hebdo
SHIRLEY TEMPLE
2F
UNE NOUVELLE DE PIERRE VERY
LE DIEU DANS LE PLACARD
SHIRLEY TEMPLE

cinegramas
Shirley Temple

RADIO BARCELONA

Fritiden
Straalende Øjne

Ude og Hjemme
Nr. 27
35
Pengeuddelingen fortsættes

Rose Fran
Le Journal de la Française
Chapeaux de printemps au tricot

A SCENA MUDA
N. 882 — 50.º do 17.º ANNO
15 de Fevereiro de 1938
Shirley Temple

CINE-MUNDIAL
ENERO 1937
30 Cts.

Lektyr
Gott Nytt År!

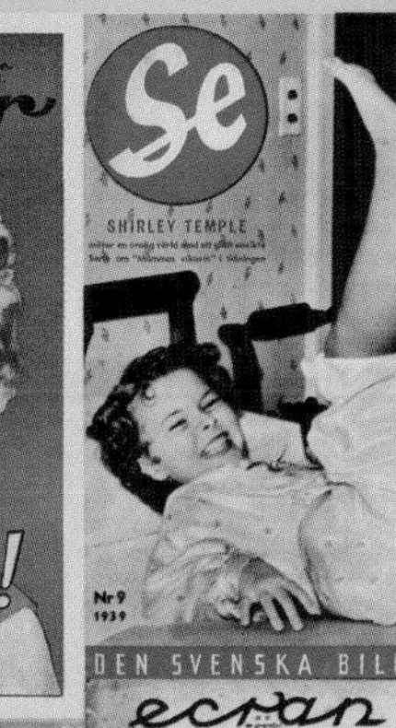
Se
SHIRLEY TEMPLE
Nr 9 1939
35 öre
DEN SVENSKA BILDTIDNINGEN

好萊塢
第七期

Le Samedi 10¢
LE MAGAZINE NATIONAL DES CANADIENS

HEFT 27
Radio Welt
30 Groschen
SHIRLEY TEMPLE

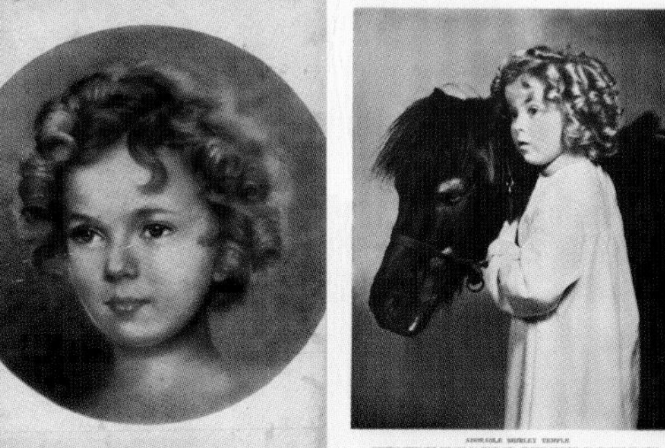
ecran
SHIRLEY TEMPLE

ALL SWANK AND NO HEART! GRAND LONG COMPLETE NOVEL WITHIN
BETTY'S PAPER 2d
EVERY FRIDAY
HERE'S SHIRLEY!
She Tells You Her Own Life Story Inside!

L'Abeille
Shirley Temple

КАРТИННА ГАЛЕРИЯ
ИЛЮСТРОВАНО МЕСЕЧНО СПИСАНИЕ ЗА ДЕЦА И ЮНОШИ
ШЪРЛЕЙ ТЕМПЪЛЪ

ROMANZI E RACCONTI PER I RAGAZZI
NOVELLINO

PICCOLA

ZONDAGSVRIEND

VECKO-REVYN
Shirley Temple

SHIRLEY TEMPLE SOUVENIR NUMBER!
WOMAN'S COMPANION 2d
FREE
ALL ABOUT
Shirley Temple
32-PAGE ILLUSTRATED SUPPLEMENT
INSIDE

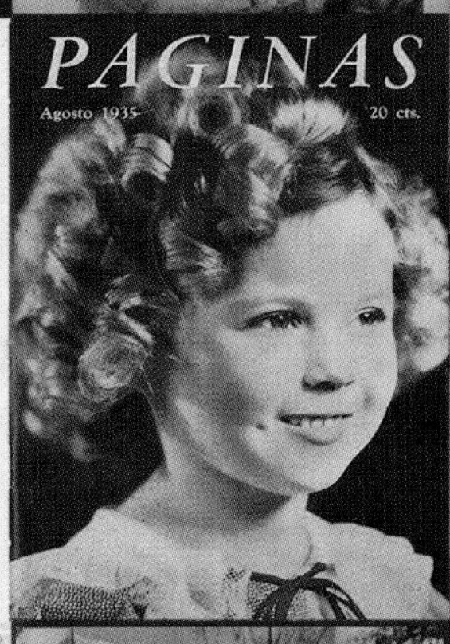
PAGINAS
Agosto 1935
20 cts.

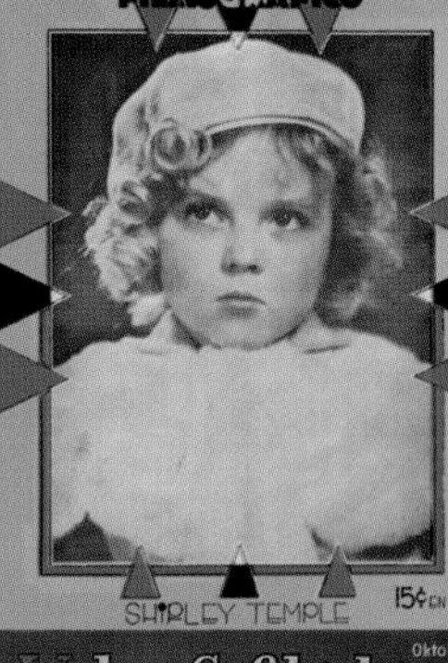
FILMOGRAFICO
SHIRLEY TEMPLE
15¢

DEPORTES
15¢
SHIRLEY QUIERE QUE SANTA CLAUS
LE TRAIGA UNOS QUINTUPLES
THE JAPAN TIMES & MAIL
Introducing:
THE LEADING PREFECTURES
OF JAPAN

Cinelandia

Cine-Jornal

Cinema Illustrazione
presenta
SHIRLEY TEMPLE

Nr 27-28

scenen
50 öre
jul- och nyårsafton

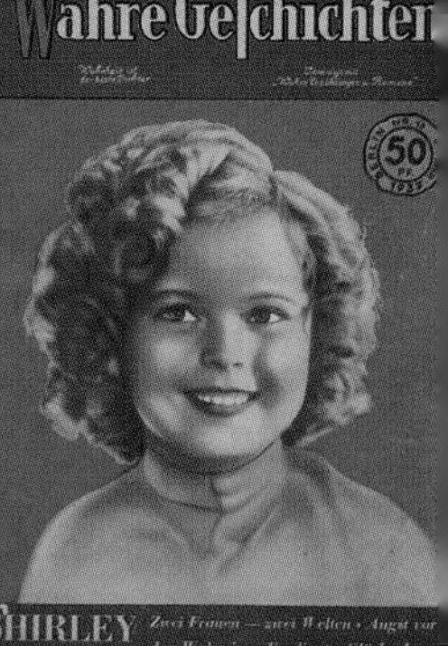
Wahre Geschichten
50
SHIRLEY TEMPLE
Zwei Frauen — zwei Welten

GRAND MARSHAL
Rose Bowl Parade
Daddie is under Float -
GRAND MARSHAL

# Queen of Children

"Will I get a badge?" Shirley could have asked that question after Lathrop Teischman, President of the Tournament of Roses Association pitched the idea of Shirley serving as the youngest Grand Marshal in the Rose Parade's 50-year history. Sitting atop a bloom-bedecked float like royalty was intriguing, but an official badge with trailing streamers was something else altogether. Shirley got her badge, and the Rose Parade got Shirley.

The parade was held on January 2, 1939, the year Shirley turned 11. The fact that she was leading the event was front page news; scores of fans turned out to see her as she moved slowly down the street, dressed in white fur and perched on a rose covered throne with her dad and Grif hidden underneath the flowers. It was said that she waved so enthusiastically to the crowds that she couldn't raise her arm for days. Photographs and programs from her first Rose Parade appearance were treasured souvenirs for fans; Shirley repeated her role as Grand Marshal at the parade's 100th Anniversary in 1989 and again in 1999.

By the time Shirley was seven, she was gathering more honors and citations than most people achieve in a lifetime. After her role in

*The Little Colonel*, American Legion posts across the country fell in line to christen her as an honorary Colonel, all with the appropriate certificates and badges. She was made an official Kentucky Colonel, home to the original book character. The Junior Veterans of Foreign Wars made her a cadet, issuing a scaled down uniform; this honor was preserved in a variety of icons, including a deck of cards. She was made Mascot to the Chilean Navy, junior chairperson for the Humane Society's Be Kind to Animals Week and was photographed holding the Jonker Diamond (the world's largest uncut stone at the time) with the implication that these were the world's two most precious gems.

**Above: Shirley is presented with her ribbon; top: Lathrop Teischman, President of the Tournament of Roses Association, makes the cover of the *Record of Sigma Alpha Epsilon* with his youngest Grand Marshal in May 1939.**

Some of the most visible honors of Shirley's childhood were her special Oscar, putting her hand and footprints in the forecourt of Graumans Chinese Theatre, being made a Rangerette for the Texas Centennial in 1936, an American Red Cross appeal made via a public-service-style movie trailer and the National Gold Star Mothers Child of Peace. When she was insured by Lloyd's of London at age six, she posed with the official document that stated the policy to be null and void should Shirley expire while intoxicated!

CHICAGO TIMES
SHIRLEY TEMPLE CLUB
REGISTERED MEMBER
MARGARET ENGEL
2502 N. LAWNDALE AVE.
Shirley Temple
CHICAGO TIMES
SHIRLEY TEMPLE CLUB
Extra! SEE SHIRLEY TEMPLE FOOTPRINTED! Chinese Forecourt 7 P.M. Tonight!
SEE BILL ROBINSON'S STAIR DANCE on the Stage! Chinese 7:45, Loew's 9:30 P.M. TONIGHT!
LOS ANGELES
Surrenders
...To The CONQUEROR of A MILLION HEARTS... In her Happiest Story!
Shirley
TEMPLE
Lionel
BARRYMORE
In Annie Fellows Johnston's Famous Story of Love and Happiness...
The LITTLE COLONEL
FOX FILM with
BILL ROBINSON
Evelyn Venable • John Lodge
Directed by David Butler
Plus WALT DISNEY presents MICKEY MOUSE in..."MICKEY'S SERVICE STATION"
Grauman's CHINESE
LOEW'S STATE
KIDS! Free Photos of SHIRLEY!
Sunday Express
Shirley Temple Club
SHIRLEY TEMPLE
the World Peace Child, Christened By the United Mothers World Peace Movement: Inc.
"PEACE EDUCATION MUST PRECEDE DISARMAMENT
Mothers
NEW THEATRE-WFBR
SHIRLEY TEMPLE CLUB

Shirley's first official premiere was for *Wee Willie Winkie* in 1937. Nothing was spared to present the film in classic Hollywood style—complete with a "red carpet parade" with Shirley and her proud parents, fans sitting in special bleachers arrayed to watch the arrival of celebrities, searchlights, a large doll house used to display her toys for the crowds—even a sundae named for the film. Eddie Cantor, above, interviewed the star in her first radio appearance over the Mutual Broadcasting System; she was thrilled to have gotten her report card and an opportunity to stay up late!

This impressive statue of Shirley and co-star Victor McLaglen was installed near the theater.

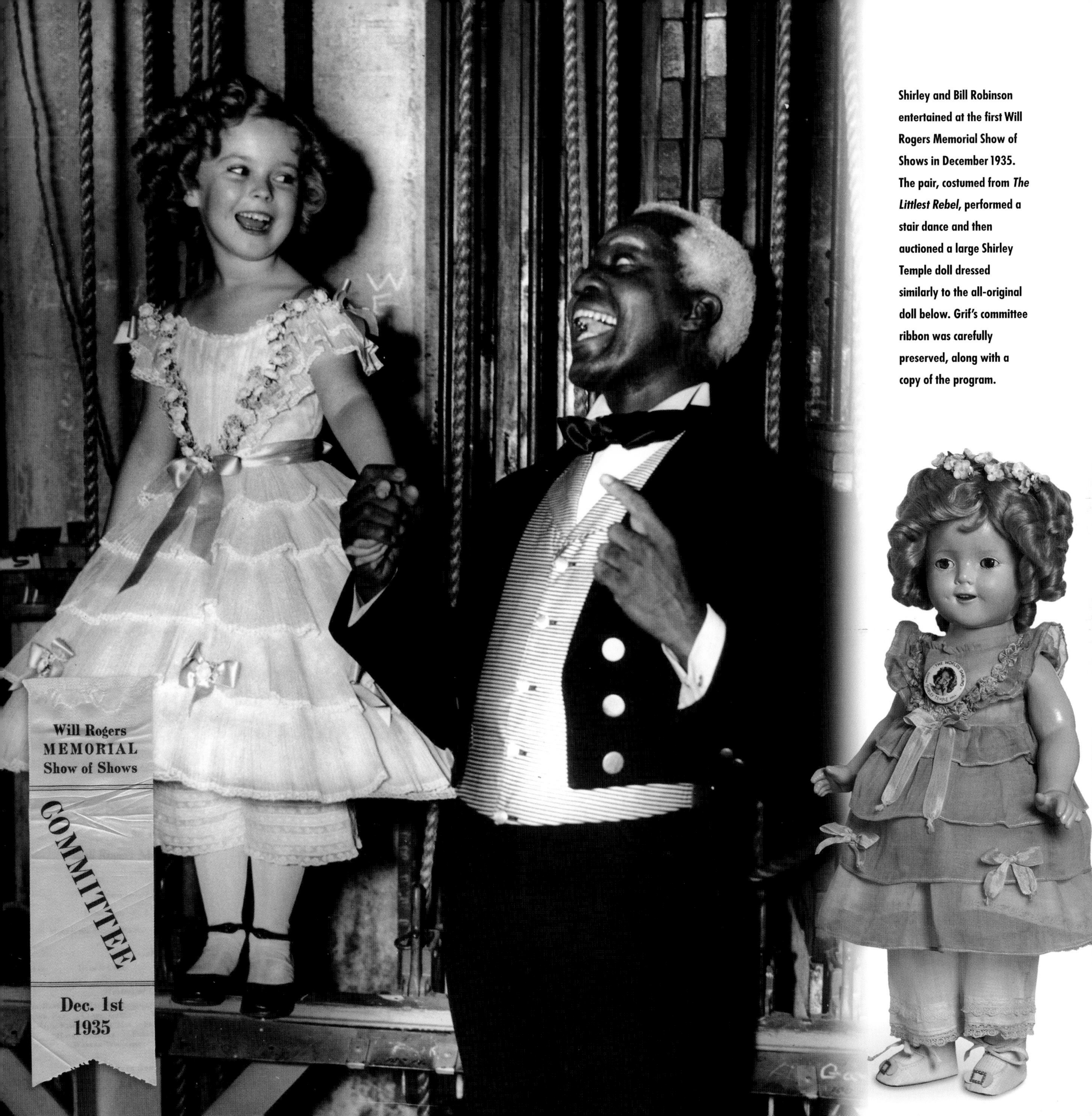


Shirley and Bill Robinson entertained at the first Will Rogers Memorial Show of Shows in December 1935. The pair, costumed from *The Littlest Rebel*, performed a stair dance and then auctioned a large Shirley Temple doll dressed similarly to the all-original doll below. Grif's committee ribbon was carefully preserved, along with a copy of the program.

Shirley's role as an honorary Texas Ranger for the Centennial Exposition in 1936 included a few custom cowboy outfits, a special doll by Ideal, a plaster souvenir figure and a cloth doll by the Blossom company.

THIS IS
TILLIE'S PLAYMATE
"DINAH"
SHIRLEY TEMPLE'S
GUERNSEY CALF
"TILLIE TEMPLE"
of
Tillamook
The National
HUMANE
REVIEW
MARCH
1936
The Little Colonel (Shirley Temple) Takes Command of the Junior Division for Kindness Week
BE KIND TO ANIMALS ANNIVERSARY, APRIL 19-25, HUMANE SUNDAY,
SHIRLEY TEMPLE'S PET LAMB
International
Shirley has a little lamb
Its fleece is white as snow
And everywhere that Shirley goes
CARNATION


**Shirley had many unique pets presented to her during her career, including Tillie Temple from the Tillamook Dairy and a prize trotter from the Carnation [Milk] stables, below.**

**The Humane Society of America promoted Shirley to Honorary Junior Chairman of Be Kind to Animals Week during April 1936. The glass lantern slide, below, was one of a set of six that was used in theaters to promote the event.**

**Shirley's 1936 American Red Cross movie trailer, *For Their Sake,* raised awareness for the charity's work in flood-ravaged areas across the East in the mid-1930s. The doll, below, was hand dressed at the time with a very close copy of Shirley's official Red Cross uniform.**

*Official*

# PROGRAM

EIGHTEENTH ANNUAL CONVENTION

**AMERICAN LEGION**

DEPARTMENT *of* CALIFORNIA

1 9 3 6

Legion events (clockwise from above): Shirley graces the cover of the American Legion's 1936 California convention program; receiving her commission in 1935 from Colonel Reginald Barlow of Legion Post 43, Hollywood; lunch at the studio with national auxiliary president Mrs. Malcolm Douglas and actor Jean Hersholt.

In 1938, Shirley was made sponsor of National Air Mail Week. Here, Los Angeles Postmistress Mary D. Briggs presents an official document; Shirley's drawing at right was reproduced as a poster and in countless newspapers—although at least one reporter remarked that Shirley's plane looked like a "huge flying fish."

Presenting the coveted Eagle Scout badge to Southern California Boy Scouts in 1936 was one of the many civic activities performed by Shirley during her Fox Studio career. Co-hosting the luncheon event with Mrs. Frank Merriam, wife of the Governor of California, existing newsreel footage shows that Shirley handled her duties with an unmistakably regal grace.

SHIRLEY TEMPLE AIDS IN CEREMONY

Shirley Temple, diminutive screen actress, presents Scout Paul Kennedy, Jr., with his Eagle badge while Mrs. Frank Merriam, wife of the Governor, looks on. Others of the twenty-four Boy Scouts who received highest awards yesterday stand by.

THE COMPANY WILL APPRECIATE SUGGESTIONS FROM ITS PATRONS CONCERNING ITS SERVICE

1201-S

WESTERN UNION

CLASS OF SERVICE

This is a full-rate Telegram or Cablegram unless its deferred character is indicated by a suitable symbol above or preceding the address.

R. B. WHITE PRESIDENT

NEWCOMB CARLTON CHAIRMAN OF THE BOARD

J. C. WILLEVER FIRST VICE-PRESIDENT

SYMBOLS
DL = Day Letter
SER = Serial
NM = Night Message
NL = Night Letter
CDE = Code Cable
LC = Deferred Cable
NLT = Cable Night Letter
Ship Radiogram

The filing time shown in the date line on telegrams and day letters is Standard Time at point of origin. Time of receipt is Standard Time at point of destination.

Received at 270 So. Garey, Pomona, Calif. TELEPHONE 1121

1936 SEP 15 PM 8 12

MINUTES IN TRANSIT
FULL-RATE | DAY LETTER

S123 35 NL=WUX LOSANGELES CALIF 15

MRS C B AFFLERBAUGH=

I WANT TO PERSONALLY CONGRATULATE THE BOYS OF CALIFORNIA WHO HAVE BEEN MADE EAGLE SCOUTS WILL YOU HAVE LUNCH WITH ME SATURDAY MORNING AT ELEVEN OCLOCK SEPTEMBER NINETEENTH AT TWENTIETH CENTURY FOX STUDIOS IN BEVERLYHILLS=

SHIRLEY TEMPLE.

THERE IS NO DEPENDABLE SUBSTITUTE FOR WESTERN UNION TIME

MOONTA CENTENARY
CELEBRATIONS 1936

QUEEN OF CHILDREN

"Queen of Children" was the title bestowed upon Shirley by an Australian charity organization in 1936. There was no need to identify her by name on this fundraising festival badge; a familiar smiling image was all that was needed.

Worldwide fan clubs from the United States, Holland, France, Romania, Hungary and Czechoslovakia are represented here. Below: "The Templers" was a *Screen Play* magazine-sponsored club for kids; members living in the Los Angeles area were often lucky enough to meet their idol for lunch at the studio. Here, Shirley entertains Jackie Smalley (left), first member of the group, and Noel Oliver, club president for May 1936.

CUADERNITOS SHIRLEY TEMPLE
Nº1
30 cts
MON AMIE
SHIRLEY TEMPLE
SHIRLEY TEMPLE
STK
KLUB
Club Shirley Temple
SHIRLEY TEMPLE CLUB
MEMBRE ACTIF
Shirley Temple
UGEBLADET
16 AARG. NO.39
SØNDAG 27 SEPT.
Alle Børn: BLIV MEDLEM AF SHIRLEY TEMPLE-KLUBBEN
SHIRLEY TEMPLE KLUBBEN
UGEBLADET
For League Members Only
"SUNDAY REFEREE"
SHIRLEY TEMPLE LEAGUE
RULES for MEMBERS
CLUB
SHIRLEY TEMPLE
Onze Shirley
maandblad met plaatjes voor de leden der Ned. Shirley Temple-Club, onder leiding van Luc. Willink.
ONDER VOORZITTERSCHAP VAN W. J. ECKHARDT
To the Dutch Shirley Temple Club
Love, Shirley Temple
Ned. Shirley Temple Club
Dear Shirley! Many happy returns of the Day wished by the Members of the Shirley Temple-Club in Holland!
NED. SHIRLEY TEMPLE CLUB
Shirley Temple zond ons deze foto met eigen bijschrift.
houdt zij de grote verjaarsbrief, die jullie haar hebt geschreven.
SHIRLEY TEMPLE v'a trimis cadouri de Paşti!
"SUNDAY REFEREE"
SHIRLEY TEMPLE LEAGUE
Sunday Referee
Shirley Temple League
Shirley Temple League
This is to certify that
Francis Hall
of Georgetown, Dumfries
has been enrolled a member of the Sunday Referee Shirley Temple League, and that she will be entitled to all the privileges accorded to members of the League.
Shirley Temple
PRESIDE
Date 13th November 1936
Sunday Referee, 17, Tudor Street, London, E.C.4.

Happy Birthday 5 Year Old
Joyeux Noël. Pendant que le Père Noël se restaure, prenons un acompte!...
BINKIE STUART
POUR VOUS
LE PLUS GRAND HEBDOMA
DU CINÉMA
BOLLETTINO DEI DISCHI
Columbia
NOVITÀ D'APRILE
LA PICCOLA MIRANDA, MERAVIGLIOSA SINCRONIZZATRICE DI SHIRLEY TEMPLE
ANNO V · N. 4
APRILE 1937 · XV
MILANO
SPEDIZ. IN ABBON. POSTALE MENSILE
Direttore resp. F. AUTERI

# Lookalikes

Shirley's popularity led to what was probably the largest influx of child actors in Hollywood history—so much so, that casting directors eventually had to beg parents not to have their daughters imitate Shirley, but to be themselves in the quest for a new and different child talent. No matter. All over the world, little girls and their moms preferred the Shirley look—if not to lead to movie stardom, at least to make their daughters feel like stars in their own neighborhood. Girls endured permanent waves, rubber curlers, dancing and singing lessons, and short Shirley dresses in the cold weather. Some actually attained some degree of fame in their cities through dance recitals and Shirley Temple lookalike contests. Little girls dutifully posed for portraits in their curls and Cinderella frocks, sometimes with spectacular results.

The most famous of the Shirley wannabes were not based in America. Successful British child star Binkie Stuart had her own fan following, and Ginnette Marboeuf-Hoyet of France—a Shirley Temple resemblance winner who actually traveled to Hollywood to meet her idol. Ginnette lived the fantasy, even if only briefly, of many kids who wanted nothing more than to move to California and have Shirley be their best friend. One strange and lovely example of a foreign Shirley lookalike is a beautiful print from Japan, showing an exact rendering of an early Shirley pose—complete with Asian features.

A Shirley Temple contest on stage presented a group of young wannabes, dazed by the footlights. Above center: Vasser Waver curlers guaranteed that one's daughter (and her doll) could look like Shirley after using their "comfortable" rubber wavers.

Modern Hair Styling for Children
by R. Louie

SPECIAL This Week
The Regular Poyner Wave for Adults
Now $4.95

Open Tues. and Friday Eves.
POYNER'S
KINNEY & LEVAN BLDG.
CHerry 2677 1375 Euclid Ave.
2789 Euclid Heights Blvd. FA. 6176
2245 Lee Rd. YEllowstone 0340

The CELLU-WAVE $3.50
"Wound in Cellophane"
Little Shirley Jones—Prize Winner of SHIRLEY TEMPLE contest.

GRAMMOPHON
HERGESTELLT VON DER DEUTSCHEN GRAMMOPHON G.M.B.H., BERLIN
Die Stimme seines Herrn
Eingetragene Schutzmarke
Elektrisch
Polyfar
H
LONDON FRANCIS DAY BERLIN PARIS
Radio-Potpourri
a. d. Tonfilm: „Shirley auf Welle 303"
Musik: Whiting-Henderson-Gordon-Revel — Text: Rich. Busch
Carmen Lahrmann
mit Erhard Bauschke Orchester
Leitung: Walter Ulfig
47246 A
Recht zur Radioverbreitung vorbehalten
From your Valentine
Handle with care this poor little heart
So cruelly pierced by Dan Cupids dart.
Tis bleeding and tender, but faithful and true,
And every faint throb is a message to you.
ÇA, C'EST CHARMANT
Chansonnette de
René Rythal
Musique de
R. Rythal et Y. Lorys
Créée par
CHOU-CHOU
L'Émule de Shirley Temple
La plus jeune vedette de la Scène, de la Radio et de l'Écran
Les Éditions René RYTHAL
Propriété des Auteurs


A gallery of lookalikes from the U.S. and abroad: Carmen Lahrmann of Germany was perhaps one of the best vocal imitators, singing Shirley's songs in her native language. The valentine at left dates from the 1930s, even though it has a strong Victorian feel.

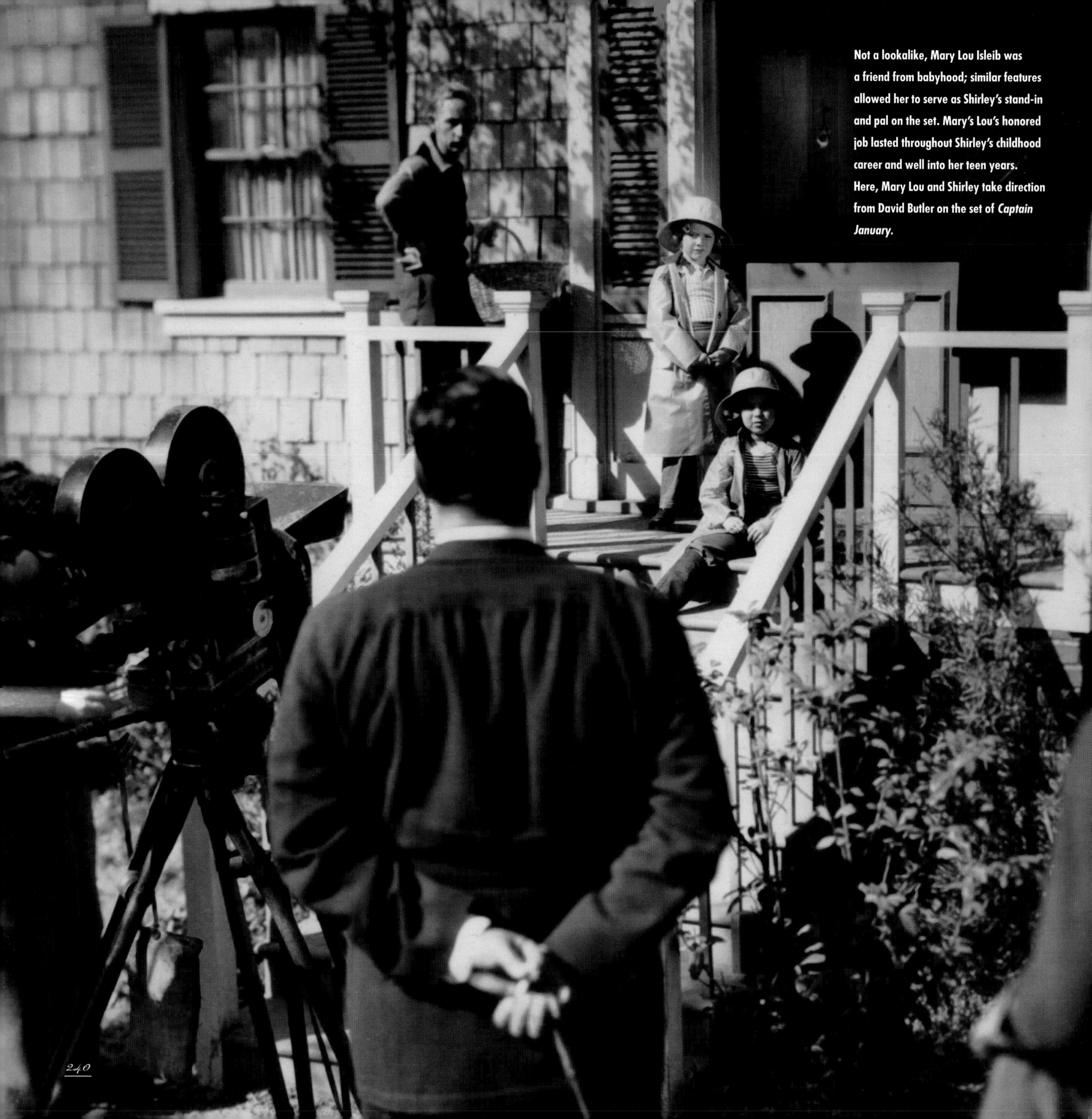

Not a lookalike, Mary Lou Isleib was a friend from babyhood; similar features allowed her to serve as Shirley's stand-in and pal on the set. Mary's Lou's honored job lasted throughout Shirley's childhood career and well into her teen years. Here, Mary Lou and Shirley take direction from David Butler on the set of *Captain January*.

# Shirley's Childhood Films (1931-1940)

*1931*

**Runt Page** (A *Baby Burlesk* by Educational Pictures)
Director: Roy La Verne. Producer: Jack Hays.
In production: December 1931; not widely released.

**One-sheet poster for *War Babies*. Educational Pictures, 1932.**

*1932*

**War Babies** (A *Baby Burlesk* by Educational Pictures)
Featured Cast: Shirley Temple as Charmaine, Georgie Smith, Eugene Butler.
Director: Charles Lamont. Producer: Jack Hays.
Release date: September 18, 1932.

**The Red-Haired Alibi** (Tower Productions)
Featured Cast: Grant Withers, Merna Kennedy, Theodore Von Eltz, Shirley Temple as Gloria Shelton.
Director: Christy Cabanne. Screenplay: Edward T. Lowe, from a story by Wilson Collison.
Release date: October 21, 1932.

**Pie-Covered Wagon**
(A *Baby Burlesk* by Educational Pictures)
Featured Cast: Shirley Temple, Georgie Smith.
Director: Charles Lamont. Producer: Jack Hays.
Release date: October 30, 1932.

**Glad Rags to Riches**
(A *Baby Burlesk* by Educational Pictures)
Featured Cast: Shirley Temple as La Belle Diaperina, Georgie Smith, Eugene Butler, Marilyn Granas.
Director: Charles Lamont. Producer: Jack Hays.
Release date: February 5, 1933.

*1933*

**Kid' in' Hollywood** (A *Baby Burlesk* by Educational Pictures)
Featured Cast: Shirley Temple as Morelegs Sweetrick, Georgie Smith.
Director: Charles Lamont. Producer: Jack Hays.
Release date: March 14, 1933.

**The Kid's Last Fight** (A *Baby Burlesk* by Educational Pictures)
Featured Cast: Shirley Temple, Georgie Smith, Sidney Kilbrick.
Director: Charles Lamont. Producer: Jack Hays.
Release date: April 23, 1933.

**Polly Tix in Washington**
(A *Baby Burlesk* by Educational Pictures)
Featured Cast: Shirley Temple, Georgie Smith.
Director: Charles Lamont. Producer: Jack Hays.
Release date: June 4, 1933.

**Dora's Dunking Doughnuts**
(An *Andy Clyde Comedy* by Educational Pictures)
Featured Cast: Andy Clyde, Shirley Temple as Shirley, Blanche Payson, Florence Gill, Fern Emmett, Georgia O'Dell.
Director: Harry J. Edwards. Producer: Jack Hays.
Screenplay: Ernest Pagano and Ewart Adamson.
Release date: July 9, 1933.

**Out All Night** (Universal Studios)
Featured Cast: ZaSu Pitts, Slim Summerville, Shirley Temple (bit part), Laura Hope Crews, Shirley Grey, Billy Barty.
Director: Sam Taylor. Screenplay: William A. McGuire, from a story by Tim Whelan.
Release date: April 8, 1933.

**To the Last Man** (Paramount Studios)
Featured Cast: Randolph Scott, Esther Ralston, Shirley Temple as Mary Standing, Buster Crabbe, Noah Beery, Jack LaRue, Barton MacLane, Gaff Patrick.
Director: Henry Hathaway. Screenplay: Jack Cunningham. From a story by Zane Grey.
Release date: September 15, 1933.

**Kid in Africa** (A *Baby Burlesk* by Educational Pictures)
Featured Cast: Shirley Temple as Madame Cradlebait, Danny Boone Jr.
Director: Charles Lamont. Producer: Jack Hays
Release date: October 6, 1933.

**Merrily Yours**
(One of the *Frolics of Youth* by Educational Pictures)
Featured Cast: Frank "Junior" Coughlin, Shirley Temple as Mary Lou Rogers, Helene Chadwick, Mary Blackford, Harry Myers, Sidney Miller, Kenneth Howell.
Director/writer: Charles Lamont. Producer: Jack Hays.
Release date: October 6, 1933.

**What's to Do?**
(One of the *Frolics of Youth* by Educational Pictures)
Featured Cast: Frank "Junior" Coughlin, Shirley Temple as Mary Lou Rogers, Harry Myers, Kenneth Howell.
Director: Harry J. Edwards. Producer: Jack Hays.
Release date: November 23, 1933.

*1934*

**Pardon My Pups**
(One of the *Frolics of Youth* by Educational Pictures)
Featured Cast: Frank "Junior" Coughlin, Shirley Temple as Mary Lou Rogers, Kenneth Howell.
Director: Charles Lamont. Producer: Jack Hays. Screenplay: Ewart Adamson, based on a story *Mild Oats*, by Florence Ryerson and Colin Clements.
Release date: January 26, 1934.

**Carolina** (Fox Films)
Featured Cast: Janet Gaynor, Lionel Barrymore, Robert Young, Henrietta Crosman, Shirley Temple (bit part).
Director: Henry King. Screenplay: Reginald Berkeley, based on *The House of Connelly* by Paula Green.
Release date: February 2, 1934.

**Mandalay** (First National)
Featured Cast: Kay Francis, Ricardo Cortez, Warner Oland, Lyle Talbot, Ruth Donnefly, Reginald Owen, Shirley Temple (bit part).
Director: Michael Curtiz. Screenplay: Austin Parker and Charles Kenyon, based on a story by Paul H. Fox.
Release date: February 10, 1934.

**Managed Money**
(One of the *Frolics of Youth* by Educational Pictures)
Featured Cast: Frank "Junior" Coughlin, Shirley Temple as Mary Lou Rogers, Huntley Gordon.
Director: Charles Lamont. Producer: Jack Hays.
Release date: February 23, 1934.

**George White's Scandals** (Fox Films)
Featured Cast: Rudy Vallee, George White, Alice Faye, James Dunn, Ned Sparks, Cliff Edwards, Lyda Roberti, Shirley Temple (bit part).
Director: George White.
Release date: March 16, 1934.

**Bottoms Up** (Fox Films)
Featured Cast: Spencer Tracy, John Boles, Pat Paterson, Herbert Mundin, Sid Silvers, Harry Green, Thelma Todd, Shirley Temple (bit part).
Director: David Butler.
Release date: March 30, 1934.

**New Deal Rhythm** (Paramount Pictures)
Featured Cast: Charles "Buddy" Rogers, Marjorie Main, Shirley Temple (bit part).
Release date: April 13, 1934.

**As the Earth Turns** (Warner Brothers)
Featured Cast: Donald Woods, Jean Muir, Russell Hardy, Emily Lowry, Dorothy Appleby, Shirley Temple as Betty Shaw.
Director: Alfred E. Green. Producer: Robert Lord.
Screenplay: Ernest Pascal and James P. Judge, based on a novel by Gladys Hasty Carroll.
Release date: April 14, 1934.

**Stand Up and Cheer!** (Fox Films)
Working title: *Fox Follies, Fox Follies of 1934*
Featured Cast: Warner Baxter, Madge Evans, Shirley Temple as Shirley Dugan, James Dunn, John Boles, Aunt Jemima, Ralph Morgan, Tess Cardell.
Director: Hamilton McFadden. Producer: Winfield Sheehan.
Screenplay: Lew Brown and Ralph Spence, based on a concept by Will Rogers and Philip Klein.
In production: December 1933–January 1934.
Release date: May 4, 1934.

**Now I'll Tell** (Fox Films)
Featured Cast: Spencer Tracy, Helen Twelvetrees, Alice Faye, Shirley Temple as daughter of character Doran.
Director: Edwin Burke. Producer: Winfield Sheehan.
Screenplay: based on the life story of Arnold Rothstein.
Release date: May 11, 1934.

**Change of Heart** (Fox Films)
Featured Cast: Janet Gaynor, Charles Farrell, James Dunn, Ginger Rogers, Shirley Temple as Shirley, Jane Darwell.
Director: John G. Blystone. Producer: Winfield Sheehan.
Screenplay: Sonja Levine and James Gleason, based on *Manhattan Love Song* by Kathleen Norris.
Release date: May 18, 1934.

**Little Miss Marker** (Paramount)
Working title: *Half-Way Decent*
Featured Cast: Adolphe Menjou, Dorothy Dell, Charles Bickford, Shirley Temple as Martha Jane (Marky).
Director: Alexander Hall. Producer: B.P. Schulberg.
Screenplay: William R. Lipman, Sam Hellman, Gladys Lehman, based on a story by Damon Runyon.
In production: March–April 1934.
Release date: June 1, 1934.

**Baby Take a Bow** (Fox Films)
Featured Cast: Shirley Temple as Shirley, James Dunn, Claire Trevor, Alan Dinehart.
Director: Harry Lachman. Screenplay: Philip Klein and E.E. Paramore, Jr, adapted from the play *Square Crooks* by James P. Judge.
Release date: June 30, 1934.

**Now and Forever** (Paramount)
Working title: *Honor Bright*
Featured Cast: Gary Cooper, Carole Lombard, Shirley Temple as Penelope Day, Charlotte Granville, Sir Guy Standing.
Director: Henry Hathaway. Screenplay: Vincent Lawrence and Sylvia Thaiberg, from a story by Jack Kirkland and Melville Baker.
Release date: August 31, 1934.

**Bright Eyes** (Fox Films)
Featured Cast: Shirley Temple as Shirley Blake, James Dunn, Jane Darwell, Jane Withers, Judith Allen, Lois Wilson.
Director: David Butler. Producer: Sol M. Wurtzel.
Screenplay: William Conselman, from a story by David Butler and Edwin Burke.
Release date: December 28, 1934.

**Wooden shoe forms used to create Shirley's costume boots for *The Little Colonel*, 1935.**

## *1935*

**The Little Colonel** (Fox Films)
Featured Cast: Shirley Temple as Lloyd Sherman, Lionel Barrymore, Sidney Blackmer, Hattie McDaniel, Evelyn Venable, John Lodge, Bill Robinson, Alden Chase.
Director: David Butler. Producer: B.G. DeSylva.
Screenplay: William Conselman, based on the book series by Annie Fellows Johnson.
Ending sequence filmed in Technicolor.
In production: December 1934.
Release date: February 22, 1935.

**Our Little Girl** (Fox Films)
Working title: *Heaven's Gate*
Featured Cast: Shirley Temple as Molly Middleton, Joel McCrea, Rosemary Ames, Lyle Talbot, Erin O'Brien-Moore, Margaret Armstrong.
Director: John Robertson. Producer: Edward Butcher.
Screenplay: Stephen Avery, Allen Rivkin and Jack Yellen from *Heaven's Gate*, a story by Florence Leighton Pfalzgraf.
In production: February 1935.
Release date: May 17, 1935.

**Curly Top** (Fox Films)
Featured Cast: Shirley Temple as Elizabeth Blair, Rochelle Hudson, John Boles, Arthur Treacher, Jane Darwell, Etienne Girardot, Esther Dale.
Director: Irving Cummings. Producer: Winfield Sheehan.
Screenplay: Patterson McNutt and Arthur Beckhard, based on the novel *Daddy Long Legs* by Jean Webster.
In production: May–June 1935.
Release date: July 26, 1935.

**The Littlest Rebel** (Twentieth Century-Fox)
Featured Cast: Shirley Temple as Virginia Cary (Virgie), John Boles, Karen Morley, Bill Robinson, Jack Holt, Guinn Williams, Bessie Lyle, Hannah Washington.
Director: David Butler. Producer: Darryl F. Zanuck.
Screenplay: Edwin Burke and Harry Tugend from the book by Edward Peple.
In production: September-October 1935.
Release date: December 25, 1935.

## *1936*

**Captain January** (Twentieth Century-Fox)
Featured Cast: Shirley Temple as "Star," Slim Summerville, Guy Kibbee, Buddy Ebsen, June Lang, Sara Haden, Jane Darwell.
Director: David Butler. Producer: Darryl F. Zanuck.
Screenplay: Sam Hellman, Gladys Lehman and Harry Tugend, based on the novel by Laura E. Richards.
In production: November 1935.
Release date: April 17, 1936.

**The Poor Little Rich Girl** (Twentieth Century-Fox)
Featured Cast: Shirley Temple as Barbara Barry, Alice Faye, Gloria Stuart, Jack Haley, Michael Whalen, Sara Haden, Jane Darwell, Claude Gillingwater.
Director: Irving Cummings. Producer: Darryl F. Zanuck.
Screenplay: Sam Hellman, Gladys Lehman and Harry Tugend, based on the *Betsy Ware* stories of Eleanor Gates and Ralph Spence.
In production: March-April 1936.
Release date: July 24, 1936.

**Dimples** (Twentieth Century-Fox)
Working title: *The Bowery Princess*
Featured Cast: Shirley Temple as Sylvia Dolores Appleby (Dimples), Frank Morgan, Robert Kent, Delma Byron, Astrid Allwyn, Stepin Fetchit, John Carradine, Herrman Bing.
Director: William A. Seiter. Producer: Nunnally Johnson.
Screenplay: Arthur Sheekman and Nat Parrin.
In production: May-June 1936.
Release date: October 16, 1936.

**Stowaway** (Twentieth Century-Fox)
Featured Cast: Shirley Temple as Barbara (Ching-Ching), Alice Faye, Robert Young, Eugene Pallette, Helen Westley, Arthur Treacher, J. Edward Bromberg.
Director: William A. Seiter. Producer: Darryl F. Zanuck.
Screenplay: William Conselman, Arthur Sheekman and Nat Perrin, from a story by Sam Engle.
In production: October-November 1936.
Release date: December 25, 1936.

## *1937*

**Wee Willie Winkie** (Twentieth Century-Fox)
Featured Cast: Shirley Temple as Priscilla Williams (Winkie), Victor McLaglen, C. Aubrey Smith, June Lang, Cesar Romero, Michael Whalen, Constance Collier.
Director: John Ford. Producer: Gene Markey.
Screenplay: Ernest Pascal and Julian Josephson based on the story by Rudyard Kipling.
Original film released in sepiatone (day sequencess) and bluetone (night sequences).
In production: March–April 1937.
Release date: July 30, 1937.

**Heidi** (Twentieth Century-Fox)
Featured Cast: Shirley Temple as Heidi, Jean Hersholt, Sidney Blackmer, Arthur Treacher, Helen Westley, Mady Christians, Pauline Moore, Delmar Watson, Marcia Mae Jones.
Director: Allan Dwan. Producer: Raymond Griffith.
Screenplay: Walter Ferris and Julian Josephson, based on the book by Johanna Spyri.
In production: May–August (with a break for vacation) 1937.
Release date: October 15, 1937.

## *1938*

**Rebecca of Sunnybrook Farm** (Twentieth Century-Fox)
Featured Cast: Shirley Temple as Rebecca Winstead, Randolph Scott, Jack Haley, Gloria Stuart, Phyllis Brooks, Helen Westley, Slim Summerville, Bill Robinson, Alan Dinehart, J. Edward Bromberg, William Demarest, Franklin Pangborn.
Director: Allan Dwan. Producer: Raymond Griffith.
Screenplay: Karl Tunberg and Don Ettinger, loosely based on the story by Kate Douglas Wiggin.
In production: October–December 1937.
Release date: March 11, 1938.

**Little Miss Broadway** (Twentieth Century-Fox)
Featured Cast: Shirley Temple as Betsy Brown, George Murphy, Phyllis Brooks, Jimmy Durante, Edna May Oliver, George Barbier, Jane Darwell, El Brendel, Donald Meek, Edward Ellis.
Director: Irving Cummings. Producer: Darryl F. Zanuck.
Screenplay: Harry Tugend and Lack Yellen.
In production: February–April 1938.
Release date: July 29, 1938.

**Just Around the Corner** (Twentieth Century-Fox)
Working title: *Lucky Penny*
Featured Cast: Shirley Temple as Penny Hale, Joan Davis, Charles Farrell, Bert Lahr, Bill Robinson, Claude Gillingwater, Franklin Pangborn, Cora Witherspoon.
Director: Irving Cummings. Producer: Darryl F. Zanuck.
Screenplay: Ethel Hill, J.P. McEvoy and Darrell Ware, based on a story by Paul Gerard Smith.
In production: May–June 1938.
Release date: November 11, 1938.

### 1939

**The Little Princess** (Twentieth Century-Fox)
Featured Cast: Shirley Temple as Sara Crewe, Anita Louise, Richard Greene, Cesar Romero, Ian Hunter, Arthur Treacher, Marcia Mae Jones, Sybil Jason.
Director: Walter Lang. Producer: Darryl F. Zanuck.
Screenplay: adapted by Ethel Hill and Walter Ferris based on the novel *Sara Crewe or What Happened at Miss Minchin's* by Frances Hodgson Burnett.
Filmed in Technicolor.
In production: October–December 1938.
Release date: March 10, 1939.

**Susannah of the Mounties** (Twentieth Century-Fox)
Featured Cast: Shirley Temple as Susannah Sheldon, Randolph Scott, Margaret Lockwood, J. Farfell MacDonald, Martin Good Rider, Victor Jory, Maurice Moscovitch, Moroni Olsen, members of the Blackfoot Indian tribe.
Director: William A. Seiter. Producer: Darryl F. Zanuck.
Screenplay: Robert Ellis and Helen Logan, from a story by Fidel La Barba and Walter Ferris, based on a book by Muriel Denison.
Release date: June 13, 1939.

**The Blue Bird** (Twentieth Century-Fox)
Featured Cast: Shirley Temple as Mytyl, Spring Byington, Gale Sondergaard, Nigel Bruce, Eddie Collins, Johnny Russell, Russell Hicks, Sybil Jason, Gene Reynolds, Sterling Holloway.
Director: Walter Lang. Producer: Darryl F. Zanuck.
Screenplay: adapted by Ernest Pascal from the play by Maurice Maeterlinck. Filmed in sepiatone and Technicolor.
In production: July–December 1939 (additional scenes filmed in January 1940).
Release date: January 19, 1940 (previewed December 1939).

### 1940

**Young People** (Twentieth Century-Fox)
Featured Cast: Shirley Temple as Wendy Ballantine, Charlotte Greenwood, Jack Oakie, Arleen Whelan, George Montgomery, Kathleen Howard, Darryl Hickman, Mae Marsh.
Director: Allan Dwan. Producer: Harry Joe Brown.
Screenplay: Edwin Blum and Don Ettlinger.
In production: April–May 1940.
Release date: August 30, 1940.

## Films Proposed but Not Produced

**Pre-production ad for *Angel Face*, 1934.**

**Angel Face** (Fox Films)
Alice Faye, James Dunn, Shirley Temple as Georgette.
Story similar to Paramount's *Little Miss Marker.*
Proposed release date: Fall 1934.
Not filmed.

**The Shining Adventure** (Fox Films)
Shirley Temple and unnamed boy actor; no additional cast announced.
From a 1916 novel by Dana Burnet (originally filmed in 1925).
Proposed release date: July 19, 1935.
Not filmed.

**The Little Diplomat** (Twentieth Century-Fox)
Shirley Temple, Edward Arnold.
Title suggested by U.S. Treasury Secretary Henry M. Morgenthau, Jr.
Proposed release date: 1937–1938.
Not filmed.

**Lady Jane** (Twentieth Century-Fox)
Shirley Temple; no additional cast announced.
Based on a novel by C.V. Jamison.
Proposed release dates: late 1939–mid 1940.
Not filmed.

## Public Service

**For Their Sake** (American Red Cross "Roll Call" Trailer)
Shirley Temple narrates over footage of floods and Red Cross volunteers in this featurette.
Released in mid-1936.
Filmed at the Twentieth Century-Fox studios.

## Shirley's appearances in Fox Movietone Newsreels 1934-1940

Footage indexes presented here are as taken from uncut film negatives from the 1930s. Final, edited newsreels for release may not have included all scenes described. Numerals correspond to the original production numbers; all are presented chronologically with their filming dates. Newsreels marked with an asterisk (*) no longer exist in uncut format due to deterioration of the original nitrate negatives, but some have survived in edited versions released to theatres.

**#25-343**
**Shirley Temple Has Party on Sixth Birthday***
Date submitted from cameraman: April 27, 1935.
Los Angeles, CA—Will Rogers unveils Alberto Vargas artwork of Shirley on the wall of the Café de Paris on the Fox lot. Scenes of Shirley at her studio party with kids, makes a speech, blows out candles, shows prize packages at table.
Filmed by Seebach.

**#25-986**
**Shirley Temple and Parents Go on Month's Vacation [to Hawaii]**
Date submitted from cameraman: July 20, 1935.
Wilmington, CA—Shirley and parents walk up gangplank, Shirley looks over side at water, asks about seeing whales, waves goodbye.
Filmed by Brick.

**Shirley, Mr. Temple and the boys of the Waikiki Beach Patrol gather around the Fox Movietone newsreel camera.**

**#26-172**
**Shirley Temple Made Member of Waikiki Beach Patrol***
Date submitted from cameraman: August 5, 1935.
Waikiki Beach, T.H. [Territory of Hawaii]—Shirley inspects Patrol members and shakes hand of Captain Hale. He greets Shirley and presents her with Beach Patrol sweater and special surfboard with her name. She thanks Hale and the boys of the Patrol. Closeup of surfboard showing autographs of Patrol members.
Filmed by King.

**#26-456**
**Shirley Temple Meets Prime Minister Lyons***
Date submitted from cameraman: August 12, 1935.
Filmed on board the S.S. Mariposa. Shirley heading back home from Hawaii vacation meets Prime Minister Lyons of Australia.
Filmed by Trerise.

**#26-906**
**Motion Picture Stage Dedicated to Will Rogers***
Date submitted from cameraman: November 14, 1935.
Hollywood, CA—Group unveils plaque [for Will Rogers Memorial Stage on Fox lot]. Included are Louis B. Mayer, Rupert Hughes, Joseph M. Schenck, Shirley Temple, Irving S. Cobb, Governor Frank Merriam, Darryl Zanuck. Closeup of Cobb and Shirley, closeup of plaque. Various shots of new stage.
Filmed by Brick.

**#28-78**

**Birthday Cake for Shirley Temple Leaves New Jersey***

Date submitted from cameraman: April 20, 1936.
Newark [Airport], NJ—Mrs. William Brown Maloney gives cake to stewardess, Miss Clegg. Pilot and co-pilot on either side of stewardess. Closeup of cake crate (dummy, but exactly the same as original). Plane takes off.
Filmed by Delgado.

**#28-79**

**Birthday Cake for Shirley Temple Arrives in Hollywood***

Date submitted from cameraman: April 21, 1936.
Glendale, CA [Grand Central Airport]—Stewardess Jewell Wood and pilot Bill Hooton bring cake to Shirley Temple. Closeup of Shirley receiving cake, counting candles and talking.
Filmed by Brick.

**#28-100**

**Shirley Temple Becomes Chum to 400,000 Scotch [sic] Kids**

Date submitted from cameraman: March 18, 1936.
Los Angeles, CA—Director Irving Cummings presents gold medal of the Chums Club of Scotland to Shirley Temple. Closeup of medal.
Filmed by Lehmann.
Glasgow, Scotland—Members of the Chums Club shown with their own "Shirley Temple," Monica Poynting. She poses like Shirley.
Filmed by Blackhurne.

**#28-463**

**Shirley Temple Drives Own Midget Car to Studio***

Date submitted from cameraman: May 29, 1936.
Westwood, CA—Shirley Temple leaves bungalow, escorted by Officer Peter Young. Shirley pulls away from curb, drives around corner. Running shots of her driving car. Pulls up to curb in front of bungalow, runs into house. Closeups of Shirley in car. Sheriff Gene Biseailus of Los Angeles gives Shirley a card stating that "This car is in the service of the Sheriff of Los Angeles County."
Filmed by Lehmann.

**#29-373**

**Shirley Temple and Pony (*Hollywood Spotlight* with Jimmy Fidler)***

Date submitted from cameraman: September 19, 1936.
Los Angeles, CA—Shirley Temple leads Shetland pony [Spunky] from baggage car, leads him around train station. Shirley signs express receipt, rides pony around station. Rides pony up and down street in front of her bungalow. Closeup of Shirley and pony; she pats him.
Filmed by Lehmann.

**#29-506**

**Shirley Temple Plays Host to California Eagle Scouts***

Date submitted from cameraman: September 19, 1936.
Westwood, CA—Scouts arrive at Shirley's bungalow, give their names and native cities and shake her hand. Shirley poses for stills with scouts in background. Shirley and Mrs. Merriam (wife of California governor) walk in and decorate Paul Kennedy with Eagle Scout badge. Shirley leads troops past camera on tour of studio; shots of Shirley and guests piling out of truck that took them around the lot. Shirley leads Scouts around the *Under Two Flags* set, marching through Moorish archway.
Filmed by Lehmann.

**#29-852**

**Shirley Temple Meets Guardian of the Quintuplets***

Date submitted from cameraman: November 9, 1936.
Beverly Hills, CA—Various shots of Shirley Temple and David A. Croll, Minister of Public Welfare and Labor for the province of Ontario, Canada [guardian of the Dionne Quintuplets].
Filmed by Lehmann.

**#30-89**

**Shirley Temple Gets Pony and Cart for Xmas Gift**

Date submitted from cameraman: December 20, 1936.
Pomona, CA—Shirley shown in pony cart as E.A. Stewart of the Carnation Stables presents horse and cart to her. Shots of Shirley driving cart around the practice track. Closeup of Shirley as she introduces "Ching," her Pekinese, to "Little Carnation," the pony.
Filmed by Lehmann.

**#30-344 - 345**

**President Roosevelt's Birthday Feted by Nationwide Balls**

Date submitted from cameraman: January 30, 1937.
Los Angeles, CA—(30-344) Eddie Cantor introduces Shirley Temple, they sing "Happy Birthday" with the crowd. Eddie and Shirley auction off cake. Shots of guests dancing.
Filmed by Lehmann.
(30-345) Alternate shots of birthday cake. Eddie Cantor introduces Shirley Temple, they sing "Happy Birthday." Eddie and Shirley auction off cake. Shirley and Eddie cut cake and give slice to highest bidder.
Filmed by Brick.

**Shirley and Los Angeles Mayor Frank L. Shaw cross safely in front of the Los Angeles Railway Company's streamlined noiseless trolley.**

**#30-829**

**Shirley Temple Drives Streamlined Noiseless Trolley***

Date submitted from cameraman: March 21, 1937.
Los Angeles, CA—Shirley Temple seated at controls of street car. She collects fares from Mayor Shaw, City Attorney Ray Chesebro, and others. Mayor Shaw presents card from city administration to Shirley in front of officials. Street car shown rolling through streets.
Filmed by Lehmann.

**#31-84**

**Shirley Temple is Eight Years Old***

Date submitted from cameraman: April 23, 1937.
Hollywood, CA—Shirley Temple and Gracie Fields shown as Shirley invites Gracie to have some birthday cake. Shots of them together. Gracie explains in a confidential interview to Movietone that she is rushing back to England for the Coronation.
Filmed by Lehmann.

**#33-154**

**Shirley Temple and Eddie Cantor Aid in Infantile Paralysis***

Date submitted from cameraman: January 1938.
Hollywood, CA—Eddie Cantor talks on phone. Shirley Temple at desk addresses envelope, puts in dime and asks audience to do the same. "March of Dimes" is the expression used by Cantor in his aid to the Infantile Paralysis Foundation.
Filmed by Fox studio.

**#31-635–636**

***Wee Willie Winkie* Premiere**

Date submitted from cameraman: June 25, 1937.
Hollywood, CA—(31-635) Stars attending premiere at the Cathay Circle Theatre. Various celebrities: Sonja Henie, Tyrone Power, Eddie Cantor, Sophie Tucker, Alice Faye, Jean Hersholt, Darryl Zanuck, etc. Front shot of theater with arcade lights. Shirley is shown arriving.
Filmed by Brick.
(31-636) Different angle of premiere with stars arriving, lights, theater sign from above and shots of viewing grandstand.
Filmed by Lehmann.

**#31-896**

**Shirley Temple Leaves for Vacation in Hawaii***

Date submitted from cameraman: July 30, 1937.
Wilmington, CA—Shirley checks in at transport desk. Shirley walks up gangplank with her mother and father; shown at top of bridge with her parents. Shirley shown with Captain Frank Johnson of the S.S. Malolo, and also shown with her doll. Shots of Shirley and her parents with Captain Johnson; shots of passengers throwing leis over the side of the ship. Whistle blows and Malolo backs out.
Filmed by Lehmann.

**#32-932**

**Shirley Temple's Vacation in Palm Springs**

Date submitted from cameraman: December 2, 1937.
Palm Springs, CA—Shirley riding an "Irish Mail" wagon. Two people escort her by the wagon. Entertaining young friends at lunch. Shirley and friends play badmintion as her dog "Chingie" runs into the scene.
Filmed by Lehmann.

**#33-311**

**Shirley Temple Gets Police Badge (*Hollywood Spotlight* with Jimmy Fidler)***

Date submitted from cameraman: January 5, 1938.
Hollywood, CA—Shirley and Chief Davis walking down stairs. Worded pesentation to Shirley from Davis. Semi closeup of Shirley and Davis. Pinning badge on Shirley, closeup.
Filmed by Lehmann.

**#33-710**

***Rebecca of Sunnybrook* Farm Premiere**

Date submitted from cameraman: March 4, 1938.
Hollywood, CA—View of Chinese Theatre. Darryl Zanuck, Arthur Treacher, Gloria Stuart, Jean Hersholt, Shirley Temple [and others]. Shirley makes speech on radio microphone.
Filmed by Brick.

**#34-252**

**Shirley Temple Officiates Sponsor for Air Mail Week***

Date submitted from cameraman: April 30, 1938.
Hollywood, CA—Shirley with Irving Cummings, her director, in front of her dressing room. Long shot of Shirley with Mrs. Briggs, postmaster of Los Angeles.
Filmed by Lehmann.

**#34-805-806**

**Shirley Temple Entertained by Mrs. Eleanor Roosevelt***

Date submitted from cameraman: July 9, 1938.
Hyde Park, New York—(34-8050) Long shot of Shirley and Mrs. Roosevelt leaving cottage and swimming pool. Shot of Shirley, Mrs. Roosevelt and young girl. Telescopic shots of Shirley eating ice cream. Mrs. Roosevelt in bathing suit giving pork chops to the kids. Shirley eating.
Filmed by Delgado.
(34-806) Shots of Mrs. Roosevelt and Shirley by swimming pool, eating ice cream, Shirley posing with another young girl, Shirley eating at barbecue.
Filmed by Sargent.

**#34-807**

**Shirley Temple Takes Boat Trip Around Manhattan***

Date submitted from cameraman: July 7, 1938.
New York, NY—Group shots of Shirley on boat with friends. Scenes passing under Brooklyn Bridge, passing Statue of Liberty, S.S. Europe, New York skyline. Shots entering Harlem River. Others shown are Mr. and Mrs. Temple, Mr. and Mrs. Rhinelander Stewart.
Filmed by Sargent.

**#35-561**

**Motion Picture Night for American Legionnaires***

Date submitted from cameraman: September 27, 1938.
Hollywood, CA—Filmed at Paramount Studio set. Shirley Temple shown with Charlie McCarthy and Edgar Bergen, among other celebrities and Legion officials.
Filmed by Paramount.

**#36-395**

**Shirley Temple Makes Dime March Appeal**

Date submitted from cameraman: November 15-21, 1938.
Hollywood, CA—Shirley walks out of house and to mailbox to send letter to President in conjunction with Benefit ball.
Filmed by Lehmann.

**#36-376-377**

**Tournament of Roses 1939***

Date submitted from cameraman: January 2, 1939.
Pasadena, CA—(36-376) Shirley Temple closeup.
Various other floats.
Filmed by Lehmann.
(36-377) Running shots of Shirley Temple. Various other floats.
Filmed by Brick.

**#36-868**

**Shirley Temple Presents Special Award at 11th Academy Awards of Motion Picture Arts and Sciences**

Date submitted from cameraman: February 23, 1939.
Los Angeles, CA—Shirley Temple presents special award to Walt Disney for the *Snow White* film short (sic). Closeups of [same].
Filmed by Lehmann.

**#38-155**

**Shirley and Folks at Comedians vs. Leading Men Baseball Game**

Date submitted from cameraman: July 15, 1939.
Los Angeles, CA—Shirley Temple and parents in bleachers and Shirley in parade car with Jean Hersholt. Various other celebrities and shots of game.
Filmed by Lehmann.

# Bibliography

"America's Sweet-Tot." *California Outdoors and In*, September 1936.

"Baby Stars Confer to Elect Ice Cream Favorite Sweet." *Hollywood Citizen News*. July 6, 1933.

Back cover photo and information on Shirley Temple's Red Cross trailer, *For Their Sake. The Red Cross Courier*, September 1936.

Bailey, Carolyn Sherwin. "December Map. Santa Claus' Workshops." *American Childhood,* December, 1936.

Barclay, Neil. "The Story Behind Shirley Temple's Amazing Career." *Screen Book,* August 1934.

Black, Shirley Temple. *Child Star*, New York: McGraw-Hill Publishing Company, 1988.

"Der Allerwelts Liebling [The World's Darling]." Germany: *Koralle,* December 12, 1937.

"Desert Inn-Seperables." *California Outdoors and In,* November 1938.

Dillon, Franc. "Shirley Temple, Saver of Lives." *Modern Screen,* December 1935.

"Disc Instruction Late Innovation." *Los Angeles Times,* May 15, 1932.

*The Fairy Tale of the Fabulous Factory.* Philadelphia: Rosenau Brothers/Cinderella Frocks corporate brochure, 1949.

Greene, Graham. "The Films." Review of *Wee Willie Winkie. Night and Day*, October 28, 1937.

Hammontree, Patsy Guy. *Shirley Temple Black: A Bio-Bibliography*, Connecticut: Overlook Press, 1998.

Izen, Judith. *Collector's Guide to Ideal Dolls. Second Edition*. Paducah, Kentucky: Collector Books, 1999.

Jones, Genevieve. *Shirley in the Magazines*. Boston, Massachusetts: self-published, 1998.

Lee, Jennie. "Why I Like to Be in the Movies by Shirley Temple." *Hoyt's Screen News,* April 11, 1936.

"Little Girl Hits Big Time." *The Santa Monica Evening Outlook*, December 10, 1932.

McEvoy, Margaret Santry. "One Little Wonder . . . and what her mother does about it." *Woman's Day*, September 1938.

Morris, Samuel W. "How Studio Makes Shirley Temple's New Picture." News article, 1935.

*The New Dynamo.* In-house publication of the Twentieth Century Fox Corporation, various issues, 1934-1940.

"Peewee's Progress." *Time,* April 27, 1936.

"The Real Age of Shirley Temple!" *The Movie Fan,* October 1936.

"The Release Chart." *Motion Picture Herald,* various issues, 1932-1940.

"Residence of Mr. and Mrs. George Temple, Brentwood, California." *Architectural Digest,* November 1938.

"Shirley Temple in Command." *The National Humane Review,* March 1936.

Stull, William, A.S.C. "Shirley Temple's Cameraman Gives Tips on Filming Children." *Bell & Howell's Filmo Topics,* Vacation Issue, 1937.

Temple, Shirley. *My Young Life,* New York: Garden City Publishing Company, 1945.

Ugrin, Anthony. "Shirley Temple As You Never See Her." *Screen Book,* May 1936.

"Up to the Minute Data on K-7 Features." *The New Dynamo Studio Special,* November 1939.

Zeitlin, Ida. "If Shirley Temple Came to Your Home." *Movie Mirror,* June 1939.

Various news and magazine sources have been taken from unidentified scrapbook clippings.

# Acknowledgements

A heartfelt thanks to all who made this book possible: Michael Messina, my publisher and June Clark, my agent for their constant support and faith from start to finish; my husband John DeLuca, without whom I could NEVER have accomplished this; William Stillman and Jay Scarfone, good friends who helped me to realize that this project was ready to happen; Alicia Weiss and Philip Parisi, who have always been there for me; Arline Roth, whose friendship and support I always treasure. Thanks to my parents who encouraged me when I started archiving and were "over my shoulder" as I worked on this; to Ruth for her patience in living with my collection when I couldn't have it with me. Many, MANY thanks to Rie Eichholtz, JoAnn Janzen, Gen Jones and Pat Schoonmaker for your years of friendship, shared information and encouragement; to Iva Mae Jones for the long-ago gift of the photo of Shirley and her Panamanian doll on page 85. Thanks posthumously to Lucille McClure for the amazing legacy of Grif's scrapbooks. Thanks to Kay Radtke of Applause for her publicity work. Thanks to Brian Black and Pearl Chang of Applause along with the Photography Department of the School of Visual Arts, New York for technical assistance. Thanks also to my friends at MBI, Inc. for all the great Shirley Temple projects over the years, and to the members of the Shirley Temple Collectors Club for their friendship and continuing patience while I put this together. Thanks to Roy Windham who kindly allowed me to use a copy of the Wee Willie Winkie display house photograph on page 224.

Thanks to the photographers and artists who documented Shirley and whose work is featured in this book: "Doc" Bishop, Ralph W. Byner, Roy Dannenbaum, Otto Dyar, Hyman Fink, Keystone Studios, Gene Kornman, Tai Sing Loo, Frank Polonowy, Reaugh, Charles Rhodes, United Studios, Ward Studios of Vancouver B.C. Thanks to the University of South Carolina Instructional Services Center and to Fox Movietonews of New York City.

Thanks to anyone I've overlooked.

Last but not least, many thanks to Mrs. Charles Black and her family for allowing me to honor "little Shirley" with this book. You are all instrumental in bringing this project to life.

# Index

Shirley
Temple